W. B. YEATS

THE LOVE POEMS

W. B. YEATS

THE
LOVE POEMS

Edited with an introduction and notes by
A. NORMAN JEFFARES

KYLE CATHIE LIMITED

A. Norman Jeffares is hereby identified as editor of this work
in accordance with Section 77 of the Copyright, Designs
and Patents Act 1988.

This collection first published in 1990 by
Kyle Cathie Limited
20 Vauxhall Bridge Road, London SW1V 2SA

Reprinted 1992 (twice), 1993, 1994, 1995, 1996

ISBN 1 85626 197 2

A Catalogue in Publication record for this title is
available from the British Library.

Typeset by DP Photosetting, Aylesbury, Bucks
Printed and bound in Great Britain by
Cox & Wyman Ltd., Reading, Berks

ACKNOWLEDGEMENT

The text has been taken from *Yeat's Poems*, edited and annotated by A. Norman
Jeffares with an appendix by Warwick Gould, Macmillan London Limited, 1989. The
following poems are reprinted by kind permission of A. P. Watt Ltd on behalf of Mr
Michael Butler Yeats: 'Unpublished Lines, written after Maud Gonne married John
MacBride' first published in *Yeats: man and poet*, Routledge and Kegan Paul, 1949, and
'Margot' taken from *Ah, Sweet Dancer*, Macmillan, 1969.

CONTENTS

ROMANTIC REALISM

COMPLEX HARMONIES

FROM 'A WOMAN YOUNG AND OLD'

FROM 'A MAN YOUNG AND OLD'

FROM 'WORDS FOR MUSIC PERHAPS'

TESTIMONIES OF LATER YEARS

INTRODUCTION

This selection of Yeats's love poetry is generally arranged in the order in which he wrote the poems, for they are in most cases intimately related to his life, to his dreams and devotion, to his moods of despair and disillusion, of serenity and sensuality, of memory and magnification. The love poetry he wrote before he was thirty-five was melancholic and yearning, devoted yet defeatist. Yeats praised the beauty of his beloved, linking her with famous beautiful women of the past; he recorded his frustration, his failure to win her love. This early poetry is impressively, hauntingly beautiful, wistful, sad. What lay behind this devotion? What made Yeats into a poet so concerned with love not only into his thirties but after that, through middle age and indeed up to his death?

Answers to such questions begin with facts. William Butler Yeats was born in 1865, was the eldest son of the Irish artist John Butler Yeats, and consequently grew up in all things Pre-Raphaelite, for his early love poetry contained obvious Pre-Raphaelite elements. But it was also influenced by earlier romantic poets, by Spenser, by Byron and especially by Shelley. He grew up, of course, at a time when romantic love was glorified by Victorian poets so that Tennyson, Browning, even Arnold sanctioned dreaming and devotion, with Rossetti adding in his particular dash of despondency – 'Look in my face; my name is Might-have-been.' When father and son took the train from Howth to Dublin, the one to his studio, the other to his nearby school, John Butler Yeats would recite aloud his favourite passages – choosing always the most passionate moment – from poets and dramatists, Shakespeare, Shelley, the Pre-Raphaelites. He exercised a strong influence over Willie, urging him to be true to himself, denouncing the idea of duty. 'Imagine', he would say, 'how the right sort of woman would despise such a dutiful husband.' In his teens Willie was interested in science, reading Darwin, Huxley, Haeckel and Wallace, collecting beetles and moths and exploring the rock pools below the Howth cliffs. He was also, however, reading the Romantics. They led him to climb a rocky ledge up to a cave two hundred feet above the sea where he slept at night, imagining himself Manfred on a glacier, or Alastor, or Prince Athanase. Shelley shaped his idea of ideal women, who, like the girl in *The Revolt of Islam*, accompanied their lovers through all manner of wild places; they were 'lawless women without homes and without children.'

His first accidental experience of masturbation at the age of fifteen is described in his unpublished autobiography. 'After that', Yeats wrote, 'it became a continual struggle against an experience that almost inevitably left me with exhausted nerves.' He characterised himself as 'tortured with sexual desire', and this probably focused on a distant cousin, Laura Armstrong, whom he met in the autumn of 1882. It was she, he said later, who awakened him from the metallic sleep of science. She was attractive, dashingly flirtatious and somewhat indifferent to the norms of Victorian Protestant Irish ladylike behaviour. He recorded his first sight of her, driving a pony-carriage, alone and without a hat, her red hair flowing in the wind. She made the approaches, telling him her name, saying they had friends in common and asking him to ride beside her.

> After that I saw a great deal of her and was soon in love. I did not tell her I was in love, however, because she was engaged. She had chosen me for her confidant and I learned all about her quarrels with her lover. Several times he broke the engagement off and she fell ill, and friends had to make peace. Sometimes she would write to him three times a day but she could not do without a confidant. She was a wild creature, a fine mimic, and given to bursts of religion. I had known her to weep at a sermon, call herself a sinful woman, and mimic it after. I wrote her some bad poems and had more than one sleepless night through anger with her betrothed.

Laura's unorthodoxy was later to be called wildness – something worthy of a Shelleyan heroine. They exchanged letters; he was her Clarin, she his Vivien. She played the title role in *Vivien and Time*, a play he wrote for her, performed at a judge's house in Howth. She was the model for the enchantress heroine of his play *The Island of Statues* and later for Margaret Leland in *John Sherman*, 'the wicked heroine of Willie's only novel', as his father put it. John Butler Yeats painted her portrait and considered her 'a most fascinating little vixen.' One of the poems Willie wrote to her may have been one asking if she had received a long letter: it is gentle and tentative, the fourth stanza diffident in its modest request.

> *How could we trudge on mile by mile*
> *If from red lips like quickenberry,*
> *At some odd times to make us merry*
> *Came no wise half of half a smile.*

19 yrs.

When Yeats's family moved from Howth to Dublin in spring 1884, Willie became friendly with Katherine Tynan, already known as a writer; through her he met young Catholics and Parnellites. They encouraged each other's writing and he wrote many letters to her. When John Butler Yeats moved his family to London in 1887, Willie *22 yrs.* began to wonder if she was in love with him, whether it was his duty to marry her: 'sometimes when she was in Ireland, I in London would think it possible I should, but if she came to stay, or I saw her in Ireland it became impossible.' In October 1888 she met Henry Albert Hinkson (a contemporary of Yeats at The High School, Dublin), became engaged to him and married him in 1893. She hardly filled Yeats's dreams of a romantic love: he called her 'a very plain woman' in his unpublished autobiography, but she was kind to him and his letters telling her of his doings treat her as if she were a diary. She was a lifeline to the friends he had made in Dublin.

Through John O'Leary, the old Fenian leader who had returned to Dublin from exile in 1885, Yeats had found exciting material in translations of Irish legends; through them he could escape from the overshadowing of Arthurian romance; he now had a mythology which would form the basis of his idea for creating a new literature which made Ireland aware of its past culture, its difference from English traditions. Parallel to his acquisition of a knowledge of Irish literature was his exploration of magic – a blend of mysticism, occultism and symbolism. He wanted to find something in which he could believe, his father, a disciple of Mill and Butler, having destroyed his capacity to accept the tenets of orthodox religion. The study of magic, he told John

O'Leary in a stern letter of 1892, he had decided five years previously to make the most important pursuit of his life next to his poetry. But though he had subject matter in plenty for his writing, though he continued to find occult research absorbing, there was something lacking. He had not yet found a woman to love, someone with whom he could share his interests, ambitions and desires.

He had completed *The Wanderings of Oisin*, in which the mortal Oisin is spirited away for three hundred years by his fairy lover Niamh. This long poem, based on translations of Irish legends, established him as an outstanding and original poet. In old age he characterised himself at this time as 'starved for the bosom of his fairy bride'. Flesh and blood reality appeared on the scene when Maud Gonne arrived in a hansom at the Yeats family home in 3 Blenheim Road, Bedford Park, on 30 January 1889, ostensibly to visit his father, with an introduction from John O'Leary. She fitted the blueprint in the poet's imagination perfectly. She was beautiful, tall, goddess-like, and as ruthless a revolutionary as the orphaned daughter of a British army colonel could afford to be, for she was independent in mind and in means, idealistic and self-willed. She saw herself as an Irish patriotic leader; she believed in war; she believed in herself as a public figure; and, ultimately, she probably wanted power; she certainly enjoyed excitement.

Yeats was twenty-three, she twenty-two. He fell completely in love with her. He dined with her in her rooms in London during the week she was there before leaving for Paris. Wanting her to think that he, too, had public talents, he offered to write a play for her which she could act in Dublin, and told her of the plot of *The Countess Kathleen*. But financial reality intruded into his thoughts. He realised he was in love with her but, as with Laura Armstrong earlier, he never meant to speak to her of love. He was penniless, so was his family; marriage was something for the far distant future: 'What wife could she make?' he thought. 'What share could she have in the life of a student?'

In July 1891, however, his feelings changed; he met Maud in Dublin and was overwhelmed with emotion, 'an intoxication of pity', and, instead of fighting against his reawakened love, thought of her need for peace since she had hinted at 'some unhappiness, some disillusionment'.

He went off to stay with a friend in County Down; while there, he received a letter from Maud: sad, she had dreamed of some past when he and she had been brother and sister and had been sold into slavery. He dashed back to Dublin and asked her to marry him. She replied that there were reasons why she would never marry, but asked for his friendship. It was the reply she was to make to all his proposals: it became stylised into 'No Willie, the world will thank me for not marrying you. Let us continue to be such close friends – and go on writing me those lovely poems.' It had been a courageous act on his part, particularly as he had only his genius to offer. Next day they went to Howth and spent the day walking on the cliffs before dining at a cottage near the Baily lighthouse where her old nurse lived. He overheard the nurse asking if they were engaged to be married. It had been an expensive outing; he recorded how 'at the day's end I found that I had spent ten shillings, which seemed to me a very great sum.' Out of this day together came 'The White Birds', and probably his memory of her in old age recorded in 'Beautiful Lofty Things'.

The love poetry which Maud Gonne inspired has to be seen within its setting: written in the 1890s, it comes at the end of a romantic tradition, and so it has its affinities with earlier English romantic poetry. But it is also at the beginning of a new tradition of the Celtic Twilight which Yeats invented for himself through discovering two new sources of mythology which would allow him to re-create an Irish identity, to build into it ideas and images he had encountered in his study of what he called magic and his extensive reading in translations of Irish literature.

He lacked the confidence to sweep Maud Gonne off her feet: he was shy and not only had he no money but he had seen the effect a lack of it could have upon domestic life, for his father was feckless about family finances. How could he cope with Maud's assurance? How could he impress her? What could he offer this dazzlingly beautiful woman but poems of devotion? He could hope, of course, hope that some day his devotion might be rewarded. He wanted, after all, to be a famous poet. Time was necessary; he had to make his way, create his career, and shape an Irish intellectual independence. In *The Countess Kathleen* the poet Aleel, after the Countess has decided to devote all her riches and possessions to support the starving people, to buy back the souls they have sold, tries to persuade her to

> *live in the hills*
> *Among the sounds of music and the light*
> *Of waters till the evil days are done.*

She refuses, finally sells her soul and dies. Aleel is bereft, though he is ultimately told by an angel that Kathleen has passed the gates of pearl into heaven. Here we have lady and devoted poet: the pattern has been set.

The Rose poems associated Maud Gonne (who regarded them as written to her), and her image 'that blossoms a rose in the deeps of my heart', with Ireland, with the Rose of Intellectual Beauty, of Spiritual Beauty, with the Rose of the Rosicrucian Order. Yeats began to think that Maud might share in his occult studies and find peace there, that she might be persuaded to give up her desire for political action. (He introduced her into the Order of the Golden Dawn in 1891, but though she passed four initiations, she soon resigned, thinking the members a mediocre, drab lot, an 'awful set' who even invoked peace, and had, she suspected, links with Freemasonry.)

Yeats also compared her to Helen of Troy, implicitly in 'The Sorrow of Love' (p. 25), more openly in later poems written after the turn of the century, by which time he had celebrated her beauty on a Homeric scale. He began to be concerned about her health, for Maud was consumptive (and had given up a career on the stage because of this). When she was recovering from exhaustion at St-Raphael after over-strenuous work on behalf of evicted tenants in County Donegal, he wrote her 'A Dream of Death' in which he imagined her dying in a strange land, buried by the peasants and left to the indifferent stars until he carved words above her grave. Maud recorded how she was steadily getting better and was greatly amused when he sent her the poem, 'my epitaph he had written with much feeling'. Subsequently he developed the idea into 'He wishes his Beloved were Dead', when she would come to him murmuring tender words, not rising nor hastening away, though she has 'the will of the wild birds'. 'The White Birds' (p. 24) is a dream of escaping with her, out of time and out of the power of sorrow, prompted by a remark of hers when they sat in the heather above the cliffs at Howth the day after she had first refused to marry him. And 'The Song of Wandering Aengus' (p. 34), so full of memories of her whom he associated with apple blossom, is also a dream, this time of successful pursuit of the elusive 'glimmering girl'.

The tone of the love poems in *The Wind Among the Reeds* (1899), however, is generally melancholic. Many of the titles suggest this. In them the lover mourns for the loss of love, and for the change that has come upon him and his beloved; he hears the cry of the sedge; he thinks of his past greatness when a part of the constellations of heaven; he pleads with the elemental powers; he wishes for the cloths of heaven; he reproves the curlew; he remembers forgotten beauty; he thinks of those who have spoken evil of his beloved; he tells of a valley full of lovers; he asks forgiveness because of his many moods; he pleads with his friend for old friends; he speaks to the hearers of his songs in coming days; he gives his beloved certain rhymes. Who is he? He is, of course, Yeats, masked in the titles when the poems first appeared as various invented personages – Aodh, Aedh, Mongan, O'Sullivan Rua, Hanrahan, Michael Robartes – later to become 'He' or 'The Poet' or 'The Lover'.

These are poems which talk of weariness. It comes from those dreamers 'the lily and rose'; it is part and parcel of the lassitude of the *fin de siècle*. The poet wants to escape from all things uncomely and broken; his heart is 'out-worn'; he is 'old with wandering'; he has been in 'the Path of Stones and the Wood of Thorns'. Passion has worn the white woman to whom he brings 'the books of his numberless dreams'. He appeals to the Elemental Powers to encircle his love and sing her into peace. He can offer her only his dreams in one of the most hauntingly beautiful of these poems, 'He wishes for the Cloths of Heaven' (p. 36), knightly devotion carried very far without any hope of reward except that she should tread lightly on the dreams he has spread under her feet. Later he was to describe this poem as a way to lose a lady, and 'The Cap and Bells' (p. 28), a decidedly more insouciant poem, itself the record of a dream, as the way to win one.

Some few of these poems reveal the effect of his first experiences of sexual love in the affair he had with Olivia Shakespear, but they do so very indirectly in their suggestions of bodily contact, their emphasis upon the woman's hair, for instance, in 'The Travail of Passion':

We will bend down and loosen our hair over you,
That it may drop faint perfume, and be heavy with dew,
Lilies of death-pale hope, roses of passionate dream

and in 'He bids his Beloved be at Peace' (p. 30):

Beloved, let your eyes half close, and your heart beat
Over my heart, and your hair fall over my breast.

Yeats had first seen Olivia Shakespear at a literary dinner in London and thought her a woman of great beauty, her face having a perfectly Greek regularity. She was exquisitely dressed and had a look of sensitive distinction. He discovered she was a cousin of his friend Lionel Johnson, the poet and critic. He first visited her with Johnson in May 1894 and seems to have thought of her as a confidante until June 1895. He wrote to her when he was in Sligo, discussing *Beauty's Hour*, the novel she was writing (in all she wrote six novels and, with Florence Farr, two plays, as well as various reviews and articles), and she was to describe his letters as 'unconscious love letters'. She and her husband, the lawyer Hope Shakespear, were 'utterly estranged'. She seems to have declared her love for Yeats, and he was disconcerted, surprised:

> I was poor & it would be a hard struggle if I asked her [to] come away
> ... but after all if I could not get the woman I loved it would be a
> comfort even for a little while to devote myself to another.

He asked her to leave home and they contemplated this move for some weeks. The risks were great: divorce would mean Olivia losing her child Dorothy as well as her property, and losing her parents' regard. Yeats could have been sued for damages. They proceeded slowly, advised by 'sponsors', Valentine Fox, Olivia's friend, and Florence Farr, Yeats's. Olivia tried to get a separation from her husband, who, she believed, was indifferent to her; he had ceased to be her lover 'from the day of our marriage', she told Yeats. Now, however, he was deeply distressed and became ill – and so Yeats established himself in Woburn Buildings. He was very short of money and the rooms were at first decidedly uncomfortable. Olivia was 'gentle and contemplative'; and she was tolerant of Yeats's initial impotence, his nervous excitement. They had many days of happiness.

'The Lover mourns for the Loss of Love', however, sketched the end of the affair and the cost to the woman:

Pale brows, still hands and dim hair,
I had a beautiful friend
And dreamed that the old despair
Would end in love in the end:
She looked in my heart one day
And saw your image was there;
She has gone weeping away.

'He reproves the Curlew' (p. 33) may also refer to Olivia Shakespear's

Passion-dimmed eyes and long heavy hair
That was shaken out over my breast ...

Though their affair, which began in 1896 and lasted but a year, may well have saved him from one kind of breakdown, it left him with a continuing sense of guilt, as his unpublished autobiography records, and as is clearly revealed in the questions that he put many years afterwards to Mrs Yeats's communicators to answer in the automatic script. Once the affair with Olivia was over, his frustrated love for Maud Gonne was the more devastating in its effects. He described himself as sad and miserable at Coole in the summer of 1897, murmuring to himself the last confession of Lancelot, that he had loved a queen 'beyond measure and exceeding long'. He was tortured by sexual desire; it would have been a relief to have screamed aloud as he walked in the silent woods of Coole. Something of this agony of frustration (exacerbated, no doubt, by the 'spiritual marriage' of 1898 between Maud Gonne and himself – she said she had a strong dislike of sexual intercourse and wrote to him in February 1898 to say that if he found 'an absolutely *platonic friendship*, which is all I can, or ever will be able to give, unsettles you and spoils your work, then you must have the strength and courage at once to give up meeting me') emerges in 'He thinks of his Past Greatness when a Part of the Constellations of Heaven' (p. 35); then he became a man and knew

... one, out of all things, alone, that his head
May not lie on the breast nor his lips on the hair

> *Of the woman that he loves, until he dies.*
> *O beast of the wilderness, bird of the air,*
> *Must I endure your amorous cries?*

Yeats's romantic dreaming poetry probably reached its peak in *The Shadowy Waters* (1906), on which he had worked since 1895, in which Forgael takes his crew into desolate regions led by the mysterious birds that are to bring him to a strange love, an unearthly woman. Romanticism, however, is tempered. Forgael thinks that mortal love

> *Is no more than a wine-cup in the tasting,*
> *And as soon finished.*

Aibric agrees with his master, and, when Forgael says that two lovers have never kissed without thinking that there was another cup near at hand and nearly wept because they could not find it, gives a worldly response:

> *When they have twenty years; in middle life*
> *They take a kiss for what a kiss is worth,*
> *And let the dream go by.*

Forgael cannot answer Aibric's advice either to pursue reality in the world or leap into the sea; to him it is impossible to see anything plain. In the acting version of the play (1911)

> *... all's mystery.*
> *Yet sometimes there's a torch inside my head*
> *That makes all clear, but when the light is gone*
> *I have but images, analogies,*
> *The mystic bread, the sacramental wine,*
> *The red rose where the two shafts of the cross,*
> *Body and soul, waking and sleeping, death, life,*
> *Whatever meaning ancient allegorists*
> *Have settled on, are mixed into one joy.*
> *For what's the rose but that? miraculous cries,*
> *Old stories about mystic marriages,*
> *Impossible truths?*

The crew board a ship, kill the King and bring Dectora, his Queen, to

Forgael. Forgael tells her they are caught in a mesh of the great golden net that is around them. He bewitches his rebellious crew, deceives her and persuades her to love him. But he has nothing for her save desolate waters and a battered ship. The birds are their pilots. Forgael refuses Aibric's request to return home with the other ship's treasure; he suggests that Dectora should accompany Aibric, but she refuses, having fallen in love with Forgael. Choosing to be 'left alone with my beloved', she bids Forgael

> *Bend lower, that I may cover you with my hair,*
> *For we will gaze upon this world no longer.*

He tells her that they grow immortal

> *and dreams,*
> *That have had dreams for father, live in us.*

'Baile and Aillinn' (p. 37), completed in 1901, told of another pair of lovers, turned by Aengus, the god of love, into swans linked by a golden chain. This longer narrative poem was another celebration of romantic love, but 'Under the Moon', written in the same year, shows how the poet's obsession in 1897 with Lancelot's last confession has been replaced by a growing discontent with such romantic legendry; he has no happiness in dreaming of

> *Brycelinde,*
> *Nor Avalon the grass-green hollow, nor Joyous Isle,*
> *Where one found Lancelot crazed and hid him for a while . . .*

This lyric, while it still rehearses imagery from Arthurian and Gaelic mythologies, confesses that dreaming of women

> *whose beauty was folded in dismay,*
> *Even in an old story, is a burden not to be borne.*

Though Yeats was still to write his heroic plays about such figures from Gaelic legend as Deirdre and Naoise, Cuchulain, Emer, Fand, and Eithne Inguba, and though *Cathleen Ni Houlihan* (the play in which Maud Gonne's acting as Cathleen so stirred nationalists in Dublin in 1902) was a play about peasants (largely written by Lady Gregory, who in the late 1890s had turned Yeats's attention back to the possibilities of folklore), his attitudes were changing and so was his style. The poems of *In the Seven Woods* (1904) included 'The Arrow' (p. 46), in which he records a change in Maud Gonne's beauty measured against the beauty she had when he first met her:

> *. . . when newly grown to be a woman,*
> *Tall and noble but with face and bosom*
> *Delicate in colour as apple blossom.*

'The Folly of Being Comforted' (p. 47) records a remark (possibly made by Lady Gregory) that his 'well-belovèd's hair has threads of grey'; he goes on to rally himself with the thought that time can but make her beauty over again:

> *Because of that great nobleness of hers*
> *The fire that stirs about her, when she stirs,*
> *Burns but more clearly.*

But 'Adam's Curse' (p. 46), a poem emphasising the sheer hard work which goes to the creation of poetry, the struggle to make it seem spontaneous, ends with an awareness that the hopes, the aspirations, the achievements of romantic love have lost their impetus:

> *I had a thought for no one's but your ears:*
> *That you were beautiful, and that I strove*
> *To love you in the old high way of love;*
> *That it had all seemed happy, and yet we'd grown*
> *As weary-hearted as that hollow moon.*

Maud Gonne married John MacBride in 1903; and Yeats was shattered by this utterly devastating news. Four unpublished lines recorded his rage (p. 48), and then there came some strangely affecting poems. In 'Old Memory' he expressed his utter incredulity – who could have thought that all his work, his imagery, his dear words could have come to nothing? In 'Never Give all the Heart' (p. 48) he drew conclusions about his past inability to play the game of love successfully, deaf, dumb and blind with love as he was. In *The Green Helmet and Other Poems* (1910) he developed this vein, recording the past, but ennobling his part in it and praising Maud. She was a woman Homer sung; she could not understand what he had done and wanted still to do for Ireland; had she understood him he might, as he put it in 'Words',

> ... *have thrown poor words away*
> *And been content to live.*

'Reconciliation', 'King and No King', 'Peace' (p. 49) and 'Against Unworthy Praise' (p. 49) record her beauty, her effect on him, her inspiration of his poetry. 'No Second Troy' (p. 48) is dignified, but, after its conversational opening, increasingly intensified until its final line hurls its rhetorical but devastating question. It is the best of these poems which contrive to celebrate her while recording how he had toiled in the hope that his love would be understood, valued and returned.

Yeats was thirty-seven when Maud married. In five years' time his *Collected Works* were to appear in eight handsome volumes. This might well have signified the end of his career as a poet, let alone as a love poet. (In the selection of his own love poetry that he made for the Cuala Press in 1913 he drew upon *The Rose, The Wind Among the Reeds, In the Seven Woods* and *The Green Helmet*, arranging the poems in a different order from that in which they appeared in these volumes.) In the first decade of the twentieth century he had indeed written much less poetry. Though Lady Gregory's generosity had allowed him to give up the hack work of reviewing and writing articles, there were distractions in plenty. At the turn of the century he had been deeply involved in the quarrels that split the Order of the Golden Dawn and made its reorganisation imperative. But greater demands were made on his time and energy by the business of getting an Irish theatre into being. It was a period when 'All things can tempt me from this craft of verse', when in 'The Fascination of What's Difficult' he could pugnaciously record his curse

> *on plays*
> *That have to be set up in fifty ways,*
> *On the day's war with every knave and dolt,*
> *Theatre business, management of men.*

The note of the love poems in *The Green Helmet* continued to sound in some of those included in *Responsibilities* (1914). 'When Helen Lived' praises Maud's beauty; 'Fallen Majesty' (p. 52) has an elegant quality in its record of 'what's gone'; 'That the Night Come' records her soul's desire 'For what proud death may bring' which made her unable to endure 'The common good of life'; and 'Friends' (p. 51) triumphantly records her 'eagle look'. The general tone of this volume, epitomised in 'A Coat' with its rejection of the embroideries of the Celtic Twilight, its insistence that 'there's more enterprise/In walking naked', is stark indeed. Decoration has been stripped off now; the realities of politics sharpen the poet's scorn of members of the newly wealthy middle class in Ireland, who fail to match the generosity of his ideal patriots of the past – Fitzgerald, Emmet, Tone, Parnell and O'Leary. Even the larger than life heroic figures of Gaelic mythology are replaced by three beggars, three hermits, and that beggar who cries to another beggar that it is time for him to

> '... get a comfortable wife and house
> To rid me of the devil in my shoes,'
> Beggar to beggar cried, being frenzy-struck,
> 'And the worse devil that is between my thighs.'

The sombre, at times bitter, vigorous strength of this new style of poetry carries Yeats's narrative skills well. 'The Grey Rock', while harking back to the Irish legends, also deals with his own youth. He addresses the poem to his dead friends, contemporary poets whom he used to meet at the Rhymers' Club in the Cheshire Cheese, a chop-house in Fleet Street. He hopes that they might enjoy an old Irish tale retold (and it is told vigorously with no Celtic Twilight languor about it) but he simply cannot keep his obsession out of it: the goddess Aoife suggests Maud Gonne to him:

> I knew a woman none could please,
> Because she dreamed when but a child
> Of men and women made like these;
> And after, when her blood ran wild,
> Had ravelled her own story out,
> And said, 'In two or in three years
> I needs must marry some poor lout,'
> And having said it, burst in tears.

'The Two Kings' (p. 53), also based upon Irish sources, is a praise of human love, for King Eochaid's wife resists the advances of the god Aengus (her husband in the days she does not remember, before she was 'betrayed into a cradle'). She had, however, been prepared in the King's absence to cure the love-sickness of which the King's brother, Ardan, was dying (Aengus had implanted this passion in Ardan so that he himself could speak to Eochaid's wife alone). The poem, centred upon the conversation between the returned King and his wife, has a new maturity, a new sureness of touch about it, its imagery controlled and kept subordinate to the purpose of the story it tells so effectively.

More poems to Maud Gonne were included in *The Wild Swans at Coole* (1919); they continued Yeats's praise of the past. 'A Memory of Youth' (p. 52) recaptures an incident; 'A Deep-sworn Vow' (p. 61), which reflects on her not having kept her vow never to marry, records how, though he has had other friends since her marriage, it is still her face he sees:

> *When I clamber to the heights of sleep,*
> *Or when I grow excited with wine,*
> *Suddenly I meet your face.*

She remains a goddess in 'A Thought from Propertius' (p. 59); though her hair is grey, 'Broken Dreams' (p. 61) carries the certainty that in the grave

> *... I shall see that lady*
> *Leaning or standing or walking*
> *In the first loveliness of womanhood,*
> *And with the fervour of my youthful eyes ...*

But he has spent all day in the one chair:

> *From dream to dream and rhyme to rhyme I have ranged*
> *In rambling talk with an image of air:*
> *Vague memories, nothing but memories.*

Some memories, however, were not so vague; when he wrote 'The People' he was recording a pointed argument with Maud, or rather a reiteration of what had become their fixed positions on Irish public life. 'Her Praise' (p. 59) and 'His Phoenix' (p. 60) continue his praise of her, the latter listing other famous and beautiful women as well as including by way of cryptic jest the names of Ezra Pound's girlfriends. This poem was one of those written during the time Pound was acting as Yeats's secretary. (They lived at Stone Cottage in Sussex in the winter of 1913–14 and Yeats stayed there with Pound and his wife Dorothy, Olivia Shakespear's daughter, from January to February 1915 and from January to March 1916.) Yeats found in him a companion whose often astringent critical comments on his poetry were stimulating but whose driving energy, harnessed to his concept of making it new, reinforced Yeats's growing awareness of middle age. In 'Men Improve with the Years' he announces that he is 'worn out with dreams'. In 'The Living Beauty' he realises the living beauty 'is for younger men'. In 'A Song' he admits that he had thought that Swedish exercises (taught him by Mabel Dickinson, the mistress with whom he had a violent scene at the Victoria and Albert Museum in June 1913; this led to her getting harsh treatment in 'Presences', a poem of 1915) and fencing (taught him by Ezra Pound) would prolong his youth but, as the poem's refrain puts it,

> *O who could have foretold*
> *That the heart grows old?*

'The Collar-Bone of a Hare' of 1916, with its suggestion that the best thing is 'To change my loves while dancing', with its desire to laugh 'At all who marry in churches', may reflect some unease at the suggestions of Lady Gregory and Olivia Shakespear that he should marry to avoid the kind of crisis involved in his relationship with Mabel Dickinson (who had sent him a telegram to Coole announcing, wrongly, that she was pregnant).

After Maud Gonne's husband – she had gained a legal separation from him in the French courts in 1905; because he was a resident of Ireland she was not given the divorce for which she sued, and she subsequently retired from public life, living largely with her children in Normandy – was executed by firing squad for taking part in the 1916 Rising, Yeats's heart seemed to have revived. He went to France in July 1916 and proposed to Maud yet again, and was refused in the usual terms. Then, somewhat to her surprise, he asked her if she would object if he asked her daughter Iseult to marry him. Iseult enjoyed flirting with her mother's admirer; the courtship continued in the summer and autumn of 1917 in Normandy. His friendship with Iseult resulted in several poems: 'To a Child Dancing in the Wind' (?1910/1912), 'Two Years Later' (?1912/1913), 'To a Young Girl' (1915), 'Men Improve with the Years' (1916) and 'The Living Beauty' (1917). She is the child in 'Presences' (1915) and the tame hare of 'Two Songs of a Fool' (1918). 'To a Young Beauty' (1918) is addressed to her and she is the 'She' of 'Michael Robartes and the Dancer' (1918). The last four poems were written after his marriage.

When Iseult finally refused him in London he decided to propose to Georgie Hyde Lees. Maud and Iseult were 'a little indignant' at what they thought his 'prosaic marriage plans'. He had first met Georgie Hyde Lees in May 1911; in 1914 he had sponsored her as a member of the Order of the Golden Dawn; in the following year they had been attending seances together. There had been some discussion of marriage between them; in 1915 Georgie had plans to marry him, and in November of that year her mother had feared a proposal. But Georgie's war-work and Yeats's involvement with Maud and Iseult in 1916 and 1917 had altered the 1915 situation. Now, however, he proposed to her in September and went to Coole to get Lady Gregory's advice – and assistance, for she wrote persuasively to George's mother, who thought by 9 October 'all will be well now'. They were married on 20 October 1917. He was fifty-two, she twenty-six. The speckled cat of 'Two Songs of a Fool', she changed his life, giving fresh impetus to his poetry, prose and plays through her automatic writing, which transformed their marriage. Its initial difficulties are conveyed in 'Owen Aherne and his Dancers' (p. 64), the two parts of which were written four days and seven days after their wedding. The automatic writing began seven days after it. Mrs Yeats is symbolised by Sheba in 'Solomon to Sheba' (p. 65) and 'Solomon and the Witch' (p. 65), poems which celebrate her learning and the supernatural wisdom that the automatic writing seemed to have brought into his life, with its assurance that all was well with Iseult, its great reassurance about and indeed explanation of his past relationships with women: Maud, Olivia and those – particularly Mabel Dickinson – with whom he had had affairs after Maud's marriage. There are also tributes to his wife (whom he called George), the silver lady of 'Under the Round Tower', to the wisdom that she brought, the comfort that she made in 'Under Saturn', to her 'glad kindness' from which he declares he cannot take his eyes in 'A Prayer for my Daughter' (p. 68), and to her barbaric beauty, proclaimed in 'The Gift of Harun Al-Rashid' (p. 71). Other poems also, such as 'An Image from a Past Life' (p. 67) and 'Towards Break of Day' are based upon their marriage, its early days neatly epitomised in the tribute of 'To be Carved on a Stone at Thoor Ballylee', the tower restored 'for my wife George'.

After his marriage a lot of Yeats's dreams came true. He had a daughter and a son, and the Yeats line would continue; no longer was there any need for a poem to his ancestors saying that because of a barren passion he had only a book to prove their blood and his. He owned 'Thoor Ballylee', a medieval tower in County Galway, and a most useful symbolic setting for his poetry, which now became more personal, with less need for him to adopt the masks of invented personae – though they were to continue and be added to. He owned a substantial town house in Dublin, in Merrion Square, having decided in 1922 to live in Ireland in the new Irish Free State. The youthful nationalist, disillusioned in middle age, was appointed a Senator of the new State; he took the position very seriously and enjoyed it. He saw himself now in the line of the eighteenth-century Anglo-Irish writers whom he was beginning to read and appreciate, especially Burke, with his gradualism, his conserving approach, Berkeley with his idealism, and Swift with his fierce indignation, his savage satire and the ultimate mystery of his relations with Stella and Vanessa. Now, fifteen years after the appearance of the *Collected Works*, Yeats was awarded the Nobel Prize for Literature, and was writing poetry which was not only direct and evocative, but powerful in its personal rhetoric, its querying the nature of life, for, as he claimed with some justice, as he grew older his muse grew younger.

Envy of 'the young in one another's arms', however, triggered off 'Sailing to Byzantium', a poem which, like other poems of *The Tower* (1928), the great volume of his mature work, suggested that the poet should be in the words of 'The Tower I'

*... content with argument and deal
In abstract things.*

This was easier to suggest than achieve. Yeats had not really, as 'The Tower III' had declared,

> *... prepared my peace*
> *With learned Italian things*
> *And the proud stones of Greece,*
> *Poet's imaginings*
> *And memories of love,*
> *Memories of the words of women,*
> *All those things whereof*
> *Man makes a superhuman*
> *Mirror-resembling dream.*

There is comfortless reality to face: man's innate capacity for destruction.

> *Man is in love and loves what vanishes,*
> *What more is there to say?*

And among poems which contemplate the nature of human history and mythologies the obsession recurs:

> *Does the imagination dwell the most*
> *Upon a woman won or woman lost?*
> *... if memory recur, the sun's*
> *Under eclipse and the day blotted out.*

In 'Among School Children' the Senator, the Nobel Prize Winner, the sixty-year-old smiling public man visits a school in County Waterford, but, as he walks through the schoolroom questioning the children, the private man wonders if Maud Gonne was once like one or other of them:

> *And thereupon my heart is driven wild:*
> *She stands before me as a living child.*

Between 1926 and 1927 Yeats wrote a series of poems, *A Man Young and Old*, in ten of which (the eleventh is from his translation of *Oedipus at Colonus*) he contemplates relations between men and women. He contrives to utilise poignant memories, to consider the secrets of the old, and to strike attitudes in such a way that the poems possess an imperative and impressive impersonality, though they are obviously based upon very personal experience.

The poems of *A Woman Young and Old* are companion poems, in which the woman speaks first in youth, then in age. In the second poem of the series, 'Before the World was Made', the woman searches for her archetypal face, a Platonic idea. In 'A First Confession', an 'innocent little song', in Yeats's words, he symbolises a woman's love as 'the struggle of the darkness to keep the sun from its earthly bed'. 'Her Triumph' (p. 80) sketches a previously casual attitude to love on the part of the woman from which her poet–saviour redeems her. Part of the manuscript version of the poem runs

> *I am not evil now; until you came*
> *I thought the shamefulest things imaginable*
> *And they but seemed the sweeter for the shame:*
> *Thought love the better was it casual ...*
> *... I laughed at poet's calls until you came*
> *And thought a common life more natural*
> *And Nature but a comedy and a game*
> *And love the better if but casual*

'Consolation' (p. 80) and 'Chosen' (p. 81) attempt to capture women's attitudes to love, the first forthrightly, the second in terms of Yeats's thought in *A Vision*. He commented on the latter that he had changed the symbol (of 'A First Confession') to that of the souls of man and woman ascending through the Zodiac, the whole changing into a sphere at one of the points where the Milky Way crosses the Zodiac. This relates to Yeats's Thirteenth Cycle or Nineteenth Cone in *A Vision*; the sphere is a reflection of a final deliverance from *A Vision*'s twelve cycles of time and space. The idea of the woman wanting to prolong her meeting with her lover is put in 'Parting' (p. 81) while 'Her Vision in the Wood' (p. 82) is a poignant impression of agony at the loss of a lover. 'A Last Confession' (p. 83) is far from the innocence of the first confession; the woman, distinguishing between love which is of the soul and of the body, faces the question bluntly, then finally asserts the joy of love where soul meets soul:

> *There's not a bird of day that dare*
> *Extinguish that delight.*

There followed a franker treatment of love in its sexual aspects in the exuberant poems grouped as *Words for Music Perhaps*, written between 1929 and 1932, originally intended to be 'all emotion and all impersonal'. In his notes to them Yeats wrote 'in the spring of 1929 life returned to me as an impression of the uncontrollable energy and daring of the great creators'. In these poems an earthy, bawdy tone is set by the invented figure of Crazy Jane. Yeats founded her upon Cracked Mary, a Galway woman who lived in the village of Gort, near his tower; he described her as the local satirist; she had 'an amazing power of audacious speech'. The Crazy Jane poems in *Words for Music Perhaps* glorify sex, comment on the glory of creation, dwell on the compulsive nature of human love, ponder on the passing of beauty, urge the need for desecration and suggest that sexual love is based on spiritual hate. Blake's ideas permeate some of these poems, especially 'Girl's Song', 'Young Man's Song' (p. 90) and 'His Dream'; others draw upon Yeats's own thoughts in *A Vision*. Sexual abstinence fed their fire, he remarked in a letter; 'I was ill and yet full of desire'.

In 'Vacillation' (1931), however, he was attempting to shake off Crazy Jane, still utilising Blakean contraries, contrasting Heart and Soul, as in an earlier poem 'A Dialogue of Self and Soul' (1927), a joyous affirmation of life. After Crazy Jane came the creation of another character, though a very different one – Ribh, an old hermit whose Christianity, 'come perhaps from Egypt, like much early Irish Christianity', was intended to echo pre-Christian thought. In the 'Supernatural Songs' of *A Full Moon in March* (1935) Ribh is envisaged reading his breviary at midnight upon the tomb of the lovers Baile and Aillinn, on the anniversary of their deaths, for 'on that night they are united above the tomb, their embrace not being partial but a conflagration of the whole being'. This glory of the united lovers – ghosts or not – came from Swedenborg's idea that the sexual intercourse of angels is a conflagration of the whole being.

Yeats had made new women friends in the thirties; to one of them, Margot Collis, he wrote letters (collected in *Ah, Sweet Dancer* (1970)) and poems, one of which, 'Margot', is included in this selection (p. 99); it clearly echoes Yeats's longing to recapture the wasted nights of his youth. The subject of sex could trigger off poems such as the sequence built around 'The Three Bushes' (p. 100), derived from a ballad written by another new friend, Dorothy Wellesley, which begot accompanying poems such as 'The Lady's First Song' (p. 102). To Dorothy Wellesley he sent 'The Spur' (p. 99), describing it to her as his last apology, and, in a letter to another friend, Ethel Mannin, prefacing the poem with the remark 'Certain things drive me mad and I lose control of my tongue'. This was the period where, in 'An Acre of Grass', he asked to be granted 'An old man's frenzy'. It was imperative to 'remake' himself; he was writing with immense zest, facing truths, however unwelcome. He was beginning to face death in such poems as 'The Apparitions', 'Man and the Echo', 'Under Ben Bulben', and 'The Circus Animals' Desertion' with its devastating examination of his old masterful images and their source: 'the foul rag-and-bone shop of the heart'.

In old age Yeats was still busy with impersonal, difficult thoughts in poems such as 'The Statues'; in mocking past myths in poems such as 'News for the Delphic Oracle', where he is contrasting the past lovers Niamh and Oisin, and Peleus and Thetis marrying (the poem was promoted by Poussin's picture *The Marriage of Peleus and Thetis*, in the National Gallery of Ireland, now labelled *Acis and Galatea*) with the nymphs and satyrs copulating in the foam. His range of subject matter was wide indeed. He praised his friends – and himself – in 'The Municipal Gallery Revisited'; seeing in the gallery a bronze head of Maud Gonne by Laurence Campbell he was stimulated yet again to thoughts of her in youth and age, blending with the sharpness of his observation and his imaginative visualisation of the past, searching questions about, and profound reflections upon, the nature of existence, prompted by his reading in philosophy, particularly the work of J. McT. E. McTaggart. His ideas were not inhibited; they could be yoked together compellingly as in the poem 'Politics' (p. 104), political talk and purpose pushed aside in yearning for the physicality of youth. And he still could re-create the intensity of his youthful love in old age, remembering, with all the direct strength of simplicity, in 'Beautiful Lofty Things', her goddess-like appearance forty-six years before:

> *Maud Gonne at Howth Station waiting a train,*
> *Pallas Athene in that straight back and arrogant head ...*

ROMANTIC IDEALISM

The poems in this section were written between 1888 and 1901. Most of them were inspired by the poet's love of Maud Gonne. They employ symbolism derived from Irish mythology and folk traditions, from Yeats's studies in the occult traditions.

Down by the Salley Gardens

Down by the salley gardens my love and I did meet;
She passed the salley gardens with little snow-white feet.
She bid me take love easy, as the leaves grow on the tree;
But I, being young and foolish, with her would not agree.

In a field by the river my love and I did stand,
And on my leaning shoulder she laid her snow-white hand.
She bid me take life easy, as the grass grows on the weirs;
But I was young and foolish, and now am full of tears.

The White Birds

I would that we were, my beloved, white birds on the foam of the
  sea!
We tire of the flame of the meteor, before it can fade and flee;
And the flame of the blue star of twilight, hung low on the rim of
  the sky,
Has awaked in our hearts, my beloved, a sadness that may not die.

A weariness comes from those dreamers, dew-dabbled, the lily and
  rose;
Ah, dream not of them, my beloved, the flame of the meteor that
  goes,
Or the flame of the blue star that lingers hung low in the fall of the
  dew:
For I would we were changed to white birds on the wandering foam:
  I and you!

I am haunted by numberless islands, and many a Danaan shore,
Where Time would surely forget us, and Sorrow come near us no
  more;
Soon far from the rose and the lily and fret of the flames would we be,
Were we only white birds, my beloved, buoyed out on the foam of
  the sea!

The Sorrow of Love

The brawling of a sparrow in the eaves,
The brilliant moon and all the milky sky,
And all that famous harmony of leaves,
Had blotted out man's image and his cry.

A girl arose that had red mournful lips
And seemed the greatness of the world in tears,
Doomed like Odysseus and the labouring ships
And proud as Priam murdered with his peers;

Arose, and on the instant clamorous eaves,
A climbing moon upon an empty sky,
And all that lamentation of the leaves,
Could but compose man's image and his cry.

When You are Old

When you are old and grey and full of sleep,
And nodding by the fire, take down this book,
And slowly read, and dream of the soft look
Your eyes had once, and of their shadows deep;

How many loved your moments of glad grace,
And loved your beauty with love false or true,
But one man loved the pilgrim soul in you,
And loved the sorrows of your changing face;

And bending down beside the glowing bars,
Murmur, a little sadly, how Love fled
And paced upon the mountains overhead
And hid his face amid a crowd of stars.

The Rose of the World

Who dreamed that beauty passes like a dream?
For these red lips, with all their mournful pride,
Mournful that no new wonder may betide,
Troy passed away in one high funeral gleam,
And Usna's children died.

We and the labouring world are passing by:
Amid men's souls, that waver and give place
Like the pale waters in their wintry race,
Under the passing stars, foam of the sky,
Lives on this lonely face.

Bow down, archangels, in your dim abode:
Before you were, or any hearts to beat,
Weary and kind one lingered by His seat;
He made the world to be a grassy road
Before her wandering feet.

The Pity of Love

A pity beyond all telling
Is hid in the heart of love:
The folk who are buying and selling,
The clouds on their journey above,
The cold wet winds ever blowing,
And the shadowy hazel grove
Where mouse-grey waters are flowing,
Threaten the head that I love.

The Poet pleads with the Elemental Powers

The Powers whose name and shape no living creature knows
Have pulled the Immortal Rose;
And though the Seven Lights bowed in their dance and wept,
The Polar Dragon slept,
His heavy rings uncoiled from glimmering deep to deep:
When will he wake from sleep?

Great Powers of falling wave and wind and windy fire,
With your harmonious choir
Encircle her I love and sing her into peace,
That my old care may cease;
Unfold your flaming wings and cover out of sight
The nets of day and night.

Dim Powers of drowsy thought, let her no longer be
Like the pale cup of the sea,
When winds have gathered and sun and moon burned dim
Above its cloudy rim;
But let a gentle silence wrought with music flow
Whither her footsteps go.

The Lover tells of the Rose in his Heart

All things uncomely and broken, all things worn out and old,
The cry of a child by the roadway, the creak of a lumbering cart,
The heavy steps of the ploughman, splashing the wintry mould,
Are wronging your image that blossoms a rose in the deeps of my
  heart.

The wrong of unshapely things is a wrong too great to be told;
I hunger to build them anew and sit on a green knoll apart,
With the earth and the sky and the water, re-made, like a casket of
  gold
For my dreams of your image that blossoms a rose in the deeps of
  my heart.

The Cap and Bells

The jester walked in the garden:
The garden had fallen still;
He bade his soul rise upward
And stand on her window-sill.

It rose in a straight blue garment,
When owls began to call:
It had grown wise-tongued by thinking
Of a quiet and light footfall;

But the young queen would not listen;
She rose in her pale night-gown;
She drew in the heavy casement
And pushed the latches down.

He bade his heart go to her,
When the owls called out no more;
In a red and quivering garment
It sang to her through the door.

It had grown sweet-tongued by dreaming
Of a flutter of flower-like hair;
But she took up her fan from the table
And waved it off on the air.

'I have cap and bells,' he pondered,
'I will send them to her and die';
And when the morning whitened
He left them where she went by.

She laid them upon her bosom,
Under a cloud of her hair,
And her red lips sang them a love-song
Till stars grew out of the air.

She opened her door and her window,
And the heart and the soul came through,
To her right hand came the red one,
To her left hand came the blue.

They set up a noise like crickets,
A chattering wise and sweet,
And her hair was a folded flower
And the quiet of love in her feet.

Red Hanrahan's Song about Ireland

The old brown thorn-trees break in two high over Cummen Strand,
Under a bitter black wind that blows from the left hand;
Our courage breaks like an old tree in a black wind and dies,
But we have hidden in our hearts the flame out of the eyes
Of Cathleen, the daughter of Houlihan.

The wind has bundled up the clouds high over Knocknarea,
And thrown the thunder on the stones for all that Maeve can say.
Angers that are like noisy clouds have set our hearts abeat;
But we have all bent low and low and kissed the quiet feet
Of Cathleen, the daughter of Houlihan.

The yellow pool has overflowed high up on Clooth-na-Bare,
For the wet winds are blowing out of the clinging air;
Like heavy flooded waters our bodies and our blood;
But purer than a tall candle before the Holy Rood
Is Cathleen, the daughter of Houlihan.

He bids his Beloved be at Peace

I hear the Shadowy Horses, their long manes a-shake,
Their hoofs heavy with tumult, their eyes glimmering white;
The North unfolds above them clinging, creeping night,
The East her hidden joy before the morning break,
The West weeps in pale dew and sighs passing away,
The South is pouring down roses of crimson fire:
O vanity of Sleep, Hope, Dream, endless Desire,
The Horses of Disaster plunge in the heavy clay:
Beloved, let your eyes half close, and your heart beat
Over my heart, and your hair fall over my breast,
Drowning love's lonely hour in deep twilight of rest,
And hiding their tossing manes and their tumultuous feet.

He gives his Beloved certain Rhymes

Fasten your hair with a golden pin,
And bind up every wandering tress;
I bade my heart build these poor rhymes:
It worked at them, day out, day in,
Building a sorrowful loveliness
Out of the battles of old times.

You need but lift a pearl-pale hand,
And bind up your long hair and sigh;
And all men's hearts must burn and beat;
And candle-like foam on the dim sand,
And stars climbing the dew-dropping sky,
Live but to light your passing feet.

A Poet to his Beloved

I bring you with reverent hands
The books of my numberless dreams,
White woman that passion has worn
As the tide wears the dove-grey sands,
And with heart more old than the horn
That is brimmed from the pale fire of time:
White woman with numberless dreams,
I bring you my passionate rhyme.

He tells of the Perfect Beauty

O cloud-pale eyelids, dream-dimmed eyes,
The poets labouring all their days
To build a perfect beauty in rhyme
Are overthrown by a woman's gaze
And by the unlabouring brood of the skies:
And therefore my heart will bow, when dew
Is dropping sleep, until God burn time,
Before the unlabouring stars and you.

He remembers Forgotten Beauty

When my arms wrap you round I press
My heart upon the loveliness
That has long faded from the world;
The jewelled crowns that kings have hurled
In shadowy pools, when armies fled;
The love-tales wrought with silken thread
By dreaming ladies upon cloth
That has made fat the murderous moth;
The roses that of old times were

Woven by ladies in their hair,
The dew-cold lilies ladies bore
Through many a sacred corridor
Where such grey clouds of incense rose
That only God's eyes did not close:
For that pale breast and lingering hand
Come from a more dream-heavy land,
A more dream-heavy hour than this;
And when you sigh from kiss to kiss
I hear white Beauty sighing, too,
For hours when all must fade like dew,
But flame on flame, and deep on deep,
Throne over throne where in half sleep,
Their swords upon their iron knees,
Brood her high lonely mysteries.

The Secret Rose

Far-off, most secret, and inviolate Rose,
Enfold me in my hour of hours; where those
Who sought thee in the Holy Sepulchre,
Or in the wine-vat, dwell beyond the stir
And tumult of defeated dreams; and deep
Among pale eyelids, heavy with the sleep
Men have named beauty. Thy great leaves enfold
The ancient beards, the helms of ruby and gold
Of the crowned Magi; and the king whose eyes
Saw the Pierced Hands and Rood of elder rise
In Druid vapour and make the torches dim;
Till vain frenzy awoke and he died; and him
Who met Fand walking among flaming dew
By a grey shore where the wind never blew,
And lost the world and Emer for a kiss;
And him who drove the gods out of their liss,
And till a hundred morns had flowered red

Feasted, and wept the barrows of his dead;
And the proud dreaming king who flung the crown
And sorrow away, and calling bard and clown
Dwelt among wine-stained wanderers in deep woods;
And him who sold tillage, and house, and goods,
And sought through lands and islands numberless years,
Until he found, with laughter and with tears,
A woman of so shining loveliness
That men threshed corn at midnight by a tress,
A little stolen tress. I, too, await
The hour of thy great wind of love and hate.
When shall the stars be blown about the sky,
Like the sparks blown out of a smithy, and die?
Surely thine hour has come, thy great wind blows,
Far-off, most secret, and inviolate Rose?

He reproves the Curlew

O curlew, cry no more in the air,
Or only to the water in the West;
Because your crying brings to my mind
Passion-dimmed eyes and long heavy hair
That was shaken out over my breast:
There is enough evil in the crying of wind.

He mourns for the Change that has come upon him and his Beloved, and longs for the End of the World

Do you not hear me calling, white deer with no horns?
I have been changed to a hound with one red ear;
I have been in the Path of Stones and the Wood of Thorns,
For somebody hid hatred and hope and desire and fear

Under my feet that they follow you night and day.
A man with a hazel wand came without sound;
He changed me suddenly; I was looking another way;
And now my calling is but the calling of a hound;
And Time and Birth and Change are hurrying by.
I would that the Boar without bristles had come from the West
And had rooted the sun and moon and stars out of the sky
And lay in the darkness, grunting, and turning to his rest.

The Song of Wandering Aengus

I went out to the hazel wood,
Because a fire was in my head,
And cut and peeled a hazel wand,
And hooked a berry to a thread;
And when white moths were on the wing,
And moth-like stars were flickering out,
I dropped the berry in a stream
And caught a little silver trout.

When I had laid it on the floor
I went to blow the fire aflame,
But something rustled on the floor,
And some one called me by my name;
It had become a glimmering girl
With apple blossom in her hair
Who called me by my name and ran
And faded through the brightening air.

Though I am old with wandering
Through hollow lands and hilly lands,
I will find out where she has gone,
And kiss her lips and take her hands;
And walk among long dappled grass,
And pluck till time and times are done
The silver apples of the moon,
The golden apples of the sun.

He thinks of his Past Greatness when a Part of the Constellations of Heaven

I have drunk ale from the Country of the Young
And weep because I know all things now:
I have been a hazel-tree, and they hung
The Pilot Star and the Crooked Plough
Among my leaves in times out of mind:
I became a rush that horses tread:
I became a man, a hater of the wind,
Knowing one, out of all things, alone, that his head
May not lie on the breast nor his lips on the hair
Of the woman that he loves, until he dies.
O beast of the wilderness, bird of the air,
Must I endure your amorous cries?

He hears the Cry of the Sedge

I wander by the edge
Of this desolate lake
Where wind cries in the sedge:
Until the axle break
That keeps the stars in their round,
And hands hurl in the deep
The banners of East and West,
And the girdle of light is unbound,
Your breast will not lie by the breast
Of your beloved in sleep.

He wishes for the Cloths of Heaven

Had I the heavens' embroidered cloths,
Enwrought with golden and silver light,
The blue and the dim and the dark cloths
Of night and light and the half-light,
I would spread the cloths under your feet:
But I, being poor, have only my dreams;
I have spread my dreams under your feet;
Tread softly because you tread on my dreams.

The Harp of Aengus

Edain came out of Midhir's hill, and lay
Beside young Aengus in his tower of glass,
Where time is drowned in odour-laden winds
And Druid moons, and murmuring of boughs,
And sleepy boughs, and boughs where apples made
Of opal and ruby and pale chrysolite
Awake unsleeping fires; and wove seven strings,
Sweet with all music, out of his long hair,
Because her hands had been made wild by love.
When Midhir's wife had changed her to a fly,
He made a harp with Druid apple-wood
That she among her winds might know he wept;
And from that hour he has watched over none
But faithful lovers.

Baile and Aillinn

ARGUMENT. Baile and Aillinn were lovers, but Aengus, the
Master of Love, wishing them to be happy in his own land among
the dead, told to each a story of the other's death, so that their hearts
were broken and they died.

I hardly hear the curlew cry,
Nor the grey rush when the wind is high,
Before my thoughts begin to run
On the heir of Ulad, Buan's son,
Baile, who had the honey mouth;
And that mild woman of the south,
Aillinn, who was King Lugaidh's heir.
Their love was never drowned in care
Of this or that thing, nor grew cold
Because their bodies had grown old.
Being forbid to marry on earth,
They blossomed to immortal mirth.

About the time when Christ was born,
When the long wars for the White Horn
And the Brown Bull had not yet come,
Young Baile Honey-Mouth, whom some
Called rather Baile Little-Land,
Rode out of Emain with a band
Of harpers and young men; and they
Imagined, as they struck the way
To many-pastured Muirthemne,
That all things fell out happily,
And there, for all that fools had said,
Baile and Aillinn would be wed.
They found an old man running there:
He had ragged long grass-coloured hair;

He had knees that stuck out of his hose;
He had puddle-water in his shoes;
He had half a cloak to keep him dry,
Although he had a squirrel's eye.

O wandering birds and rushy beds,
You put such folly in our heads
With all this crying in the wind,
No common love is to our mind,
And our poor Kate or Nan is less
Than any whose unhappiness
Awoke the harp-strings long ago.
Yet they that know all things but know
That all this life can give us is
A child's laughter, a woman's kiss.
Who was it put so great a scorn
In the grey reeds that night and morn
Are trodden and broken by the herds,
And in the light bodies of birds
The north wind tumbles to and fro
And pinches among hail and snow?

That runner said: 'I am from the south;
I run to Baile Honey-Mouth,
To tell him how the girl Aillinn
Rode from the country of her kin,
And old and young men rode with her:
For all that country had been astir
If anybody half as fair
Had chosen a husband anywhere
But where it could see her every day.
When they had ridden a little way
An old man caught the horse's head
With: "You must home again, and wed
With somebody in your own land."
A young man cried and kissed her hand,

"O lady, wed with one of us";
And when no face grew piteous
For any gentle thing she spake,
She fell and died of the heart-break.'

Because a lover's heart's worn out,
Being tumbled and blown about
By its own blind imagining,
And will believe that anything
That is bad enough to be true, is true,
Baile's heart was broken in two;
And he, being laid upon green boughs,
Was carried to the goodly house
Where the Hound of Ulad sat before
The brazen pillars of his door,
His face bowed low to weep the end
Of the harper's daughter and her friend.
For although years had passed away
He always wept them on that day,
For on that day they had been betrayed;
And now that Honey-Mouth is laid
Under a cairn of sleepy stone
Before his eyes, he has tears for none,
Although he is carrying stone, but two
For whom the cairn's but heaped anew.

We hold, because our memory is
So full of that thing and of this,
That out of sight is out of mind.
But the grey rush under the wind
And the grey bird with crooked bill
Have such long memories that they still
Remember Deirdre and her man;
And when we walk with Kate or Nan
About the windy water-side,
Our hearts can hear the voices chide.
How could we be so soon content,

Who know the way that Naoise went?
And they have news of Deirdre's eyes,
Who being lovely was so wise –
Ah! wise, my heart knows well how wise.

Now had that old gaunt crafty one,
Gathering his cloak about him, run
Where Aillinn rode with waiting-maids,
Who amid leafy lights and shades
Dreamed of the hands that would unlace
Their bodices in some dim place
When they had come to the marriage-bed;
And harpers, pacing with high head
As though their music were enough
To make the savage heart of love
Grow gentle without sorrowing,
Imagining and pondering
Heaven knows what calamity;

'Another's hurried off,' cried he,
'From heat and cold and wind and wave;
They have heaped the stones above his grave
In Muirthemne, and over it
In changeless Ogham letters writ –
Baile, that was of Rury's seed.
But the gods long ago decreed
No waiting-maid should ever spread
Baile and Allinn's marriage-bed,
For they should clip and clip again
Where wild bees hive on the Great Plain.
Therefore it is but little news
That put this hurry in my shoes.'

Then seeing that he scarce had spoke
Before her love-worn heart had broke,
He ran and laughed until he came
To that high hill the herdsmen name

The Hill Seat of Laighen, because
Some god or king had made the laws
That held the land together there,
In old times among the clouds of the air.

That old man climbed; the day grew dim;
Two swans came flying up to him,
Linked by a gold chain each to each,
And with low murmuring laughing speech
Alighted on the windy grass.
They knew him: his changed body was
Tall, proud and ruddy, and light wings
Were hovering over the harp-strings
That Edain, Midhir's wife, had wove
In the hid place, being crazed by love.

What shall I call them? fish that swim,
Scale rubbing scale where light is dim
By a broad water-lily leaf;
Or mice in the one wheaten sheaf
Forgotten at the threshing-place;
Or birds lost in the one clear space
Of morning light in a dim sky;
Or, it may be, the eyelids of one eye,
Or the door-pillars of one house,
Or two sweet blossoming apple-boughs
That have one shadow on the ground;
Or the two strings that made one sound
Where that wise harper's finger ran.
For this young girl and this young man
Have happiness without an end,
Because they have made so good a friend.

They know all wonders, for they pass
The towery gates of Gorias,
And Findrias and Falias,
And long-forgotten Murias,
Among the giant kings whose hoard,

Cauldron and spear and stone and sword,
Was robbed before earth gave the wheat;
Wandering from broken street to street
They come where some huge watcher is,
And tremble with their love and kiss.

They know undying things, for they
Wander where earth withers away,
Though nothing troubles the great streams
But light from the pale stars, and gleams
From the holy orchards, where there is none
But fruit that is of precious stone,
Or apples of the sun and moon.

What were our praise to them? They eat
Quiet's wild heart, like daily meat;
Who when night thickens are afloat
On dappled skins in a glass boat,
Far out under a windless sky;
While over them birds of Aengus fly,
And over the tiller and the prow,
And waving white wings to and fro
Awaken wanderings of light air
To stir their coverlet and their hair.

And poets found, old writers say,
A yew tree where his body lay;
But a wild apple hid the grass
With its sweet blossom where hers was;
And being in good heart, because
A better time had come again
After the deaths of many men,
And that long fighting at the ford,
They wrote on tablets of thin board,
Made of the apple and the yew,
All the love stories that they knew.

Let rush and bird cry out their fill
Of the harper's daughter if they will,
Beloved, I am not afraid of her.
She is not wiser nor lovelier,
And you are more high of heart than she,
For all her wanderings over-sea;
But I'd have bird and rush forget
Those other two; for never yet
Has lover lived, but longed to wive
Like them that are no more alive.

ROMANTIC
REALISM

The poems in this section were written between 1901 and 1915. Most of them were inspired by Yeats's reactions to Maud Gonne's marriage in 1903. In them he is more direct; he relies less upon decoration than before.

The Arrow

I thought of your beauty, and this arrow,
Made out of a wild thought, is in my marrow.
There's no man may look upon her, no man,
As when newly grown to be a woman,
Tall and noble but with face and bosom
Delicate in colour as apple blossom.
This beauty's kinder, yet for a reason
I could weep that the old is out of season.

Adam's Curse

We sat together at one summer's end,
That beautiful mild woman, your close friend,
And you and I, and talked of poetry.
I said, 'A line will take us hours maybe;
Yet if it does not seem a moment's thought,
Our stitching and unstitching has been naught.
Better go down upon your marrow-bones
And scrub a kitchen pavement, or break stones
Like an old pauper, in all kinds of weather;
For to articulate sweet sounds together
Is to work harder than all these, and yet
Be thought an idler by the noisy set
Of bankers, schoolmasters, and clergymen
The martyrs call the world.'

                          And thereupon
That beautiful mild woman for whose sake
There's many a one shall find out all heartache
On finding that her voice is sweet and low
Replied, 'To be born woman is to know –
Although they do not talk of it at school –
That we must labour to be beautiful.'

I said, 'It's certain there is no fine thing
Since Adam's fall but needs much labouring.
There have been lovers who thought love should be
So much compounded of high courtesy
That they would sigh and quote with learned looks
Precedents out of beautiful old books;
Yet now it seems an idle trade enough.'

We sat grown quiet at the name of love;
We saw the last embers of daylight die,
And in the trembling blue-green of the sky
A moon, worn as if it had been a shell
Washed by time's waters as they rose and fell
About the stars and broke in days and years.

I had a thought for no one's but your ears:
That you were beautiful, and that I strove
To love you in the old high way of love;
That it had all seemed happy, and yet we'd grown
As weary-hearted as that hollow moon.

The Folly of Being Comforted

One that is ever kind said yesterday:
'Your well-belovèd's hair has threads of grey,
And little shadows come about her eyes;
Time can but make it easier to be wise
Though now it seems impossible, and so
All that you need is patience.'

                           Heart cries, 'No,
I have not a crumb of comfort, not a grain.
Time can but make her beauty over again:
Because of that great nobleness of hers
The fire that stirs about her, when she stirs,
Burns but more clearly. O she had not these ways
When all the wild summer was in her gaze.'
O heart! O heart! if she'd but turn her head,
You'd know the folly of being comforted.

[Unpublished Lines, written after Maud Gonne married John MacBride]

My dear is angry, that of late
I cry all base blood down
As if she had not taught me hate
By kisses by a clown.

Never Give all the Heart

Never give all the heart, for love
Will hardly seem worth thinking of
To passionate women if it seem
Certain, and they never dream
That it fades out from kiss to kiss;
For everything that's lovely is
But a brief, dreamy, kind delight.
O never give the heart outright,
For they, for all smooth lips can say,
Have given their hearts up to the play.
And who could play it well enough
If deaf and dumb and blind with love?
He that made this knows all the cost,
For he gave all his heart and lost.

No Second Troy

Why should I blame her that she filled my days
With misery, or that she would of late
Have taught to ignorant men most violent ways,
Or hurled the little streets upon the great,

Had they but courage equal to desire?
What could have made her peaceful with a mind
That nobleness made simple as a fire,
With beauty like a tightened bow, a kind
That is not natural in an age like this,
Being high and solitary and most stern?
Why, what could she have done, being what she is?
Was there another Troy for her to burn?

Peace

Ah, that Time could touch a form
That could show what Homer's age
Bred to be a hero's wage.
'Were not all her life but storm,
Would not painters paint a form
Of such noble lines,' I said,
'Such a delicate high head,
All that sternness amid charm,
All that sweetness amid strength?'
Ah, but peace that comes at length,
Came when Time had touched her form.

Against Unworthy Praise

O heart, be at peace, because
Nor knave nor dolt can break
What's not for their applause,
Being for a woman's sake.
Enough if the work has seemed,
So did she your strength renew,
A dream that a lion had dreamed
Till the wilderness cried aloud,
A secret between you two,
Between the proud and the proud.

What, still you would have their praise!
But here's a haughtier text,
The labyrinth of her days
That her own strangeness perplexed;
And how what her dreaming gave
Earned slander, ingratitude,
From self-same dolt and knave;
Aye, and worse wrong than these.
Yet she, singing upon her road,
Half lion, half child, is at peace.

Brown Penny

I whispered, 'I am too young,'
And then, 'I am old enough';
Wherefore I threw a penny
To find out if I might love.
'Go and love, go and love, young man,
If the lady be young and fair.'
Ah, penny, brown penny, brown penny,
I am looped in the loops of her hair.

O love is the crooked thing,
There is nobody wise enough
To find out all that is in it,
For he would be thinking of love
Till the stars had run away
And the shadows eaten the moon.
Ah, penny, brown penny, brown penny,
One cannot begin it too soon.

Friends

Now must I these three praise –
Three women that have wrought
What joy is in my days:
One because no thought,
Nor those unpassing cares,
No, not in these fifteen
Many-times-troubled years,
Could ever come between
Mind and delighted mind;
And one because her hand
Had strength that could unbind
What none can understand,
What none can have and thrive,
Youth's dreamy load, till she
So changed me that I live
Labouring in ecstasy.
And what of her that took
All till my youth was gone
With scarce a pitying look?
How could I praise that one?
When day begins to break
I count my good and bad,
Being wakeful for her sake,
Remembering what she had,
What eagle look still shows,
While up from my heart's root
So great a sweetness flows
I shake from head to foot.

Fallen Majesty

Although crowds gathered once if she but showed her face,
And even old men's eyes grew dim, this hand alone,
Like some last courtier at a gypsy camping-place
Babbling of fallen majesty, records what's gone.

The lineaments, a heart that laughter has made sweet,
These, these remain, but I record what's gone. A crowd
Will gather, and not know it walks the very street
Whereon a thing once walked that seemed a burning cloud.

A Memory of Youth

The moments passed as at a play;
I had the wisdom love brings forth;
I had my share of mother-wit,
And yet for all that I could say,
And though I had her praise for it,
A cloud blown from the cut-throat North
Suddenly hid Love's moon away.

Believing every word I said,
I praised her body and her mind
Till pride had made her eyes grow bright,
And pleasure made her cheeks grow red,
And vanity her footfall light,
Yet we, for all that praise, could find
Nothing but darkness overhead.

We sat as silent as a stone,
We knew, though she'd not said a word,
That even the best of love must die,
And had been savagely undone
Were it not that Love upon the cry
Of a most ridiculous little bird
Tore from the clouds his marvellous moon.

The Two Kings

King Eochaid came at sundown to a wood
Westward of Tara. Hurrying to his queen
He had outridden his war-wasted men
That with empounded cattle trod the mire,
And where beech-trees had mixed a pale green light
With the ground-ivy's blue, he saw a stag
Whiter than curds, its eyes the tint of the sea.
Because it stood upon his path and seemed
More hands in height than any stag in the world
He sat with tightened rein and loosened mouth
Upon his trembling horse, then drove the spur;
But the stag stooped and ran at him, and passed,
Rending the horse's flank. King Eochaid reeled,
Then drew his sword to hold its levelled point
Against the stag. When horn and steel were met
The horn resounded as though it had been silver,
A sweet, miraculous, terrifying sound.
Horn locked in sword, they tugged and struggled there
As though a stag and unicorn were met
Among the African Mountains of the Moon,
Until at last the double horns, drawn backward,
Butted below the single and so pierced
The entrails of the horse. Dropping his sword
King Eochaid seized the horns in his strong hands
And stared into the sea-green eye, and so

Hither and thither to and fro they trod
Till all the place was beaten into mire.
The strong thigh and the agile thigh were met,
The hands that gathered up the might of the world,
And hoof and horn that had sucked in their speed
Amid the elaborate wilderness of the air.
Through bush they plunged and over ivied root,
And where the stone struck fire, while in the leaves
A squirrel whinnied and a bird screamed out;
But when at last he forced those sinewy flanks
Against a beech-bole, he threw down the beast
And knelt above it with drawn knife. On the instant
It vanished like a shadow, and a cry
So mournful that it seemed the cry of one
Who had lost some unimaginable treasure
Wandered between the blue and the green leaf
And climbed into the air, crumbling away,
Till all had seemed a shadow or a vision
But for the trodden mire, the pool of blood,
The disembowelled horse.

     King Eochaid ran
Toward peopled Tara, nor stood to draw his breath
Until he came before the painted wall,
The posts of polished yew, circled with bronze,
Of the great door; but though the hanging lamps
Showed their faint light through the unshuttered windows,
Nor door, nor mouth, nor slipper made a noise,
Nor on the ancient beaten paths, that wound
From well-side or from plough-land, was there noise;
Nor had there been the noise of living thing
Before him or behind, but that far off
On the horizon edge bellowed the herds.
Knowing that silence brings no good to kings,
And mocks returning victory, he passed
Between the pillars with a beating heart
And saw where in the midst of the great hall
Pale-faced, alone upon a bench, Edain

Sat upright with a sword before her feet.
Her hands on either side had gripped the bench,
Her eyes were cold and steady, her lips tight.
Some passion had made her stone. Hearing a foot
She started and then knew whose foot it was;
But when he thought to take her in his arms
She motioned him afar, and rose and spoke:
'I have sent among the fields or to the woods
The fighting-men and servants of this house,
For I would have your judgment upon one
Who is self-accused. If she be innocent
She would not look in any known man's face
Till judgment has been given, and if guilty,
Would never look again on known man's face.'
And at these words he paled, as she had paled,
Knowing that he should find upon her lips
The meaning of that monstrous day.
                                   Then she:
'You brought me where your brother Ardan sat
Always in his one seat, and bid me care him
Through that strange illness that had fixed him there,
And should he die to heap his burial-mound
And carve his name in Ogham.' Eochaid said,
'He lives?' 'He lives and is a healthy man.'
'While I have him and you it matters little
What man you have lost, what evil you have found.'
'I bid them make his bed under this roof
And carried him his food with my own hands,
And so the weeks passed by. But when I said,
"What is this trouble?" he would answer nothing,
Though always at my words his trouble grew;
And I but asked the more, till he cried out,
Weary of many questions: "There are things
That make the heart akin to the dumb stone."
Then I replied, "Although you hide a secret,
Hopeless and dear, or terrible to think on,
Speak it, that I may send through the wide world

For medicine." Thereon he cried aloud,
"Day after day you question me, and I,
Because there is such a storm amid my thoughts
I shall be carried in the gust, command,
Forbid, beseech and waste my breath." Then I:
"Although the thing that you have hid were evil,
The speaking of it could be no great wrong,
And evil must it be, if done 'twere worse
Than mound and stone that keep all virtue in,
And loosen on us dreams that waste our life,
Shadows and shows that can but turn the brain."
But finding him still silent I stooped down
And whispering that none but he should hear,
Said, "If a woman has put this on you,
My men, whether it please her or displease,
And though they have to cross the Loughlan waters
And take her in the middle of armed men,
Shall make her look upon her handiwork,
That she may quench the rick she has fired; and though
She may have worn silk clothes, or worn a crown,
She'll not be proud, knowing within her heart
That our sufficient portion of the world
Is that we give, although it be brief giving,
Happiness to children and to men."
Then he, driven by his thought beyond his thought,
And speaking what he would not though he would,
Sighed, "You, even you yourself, could work the cure!"
And at those words I rose and I went out
And for nine days he had food from other hands,
And for nine days my mind went whirling round
The one disastrous zodiac, muttering
That the immedicable mound's beyond
Our questioning, beyond our pity even.
But when nine days had gone I stood again
Before his chair and bending down my head
I bade him go when all his household slept
To an old empty woodman's house that's hidden

Westward of Tara, among the hazel-trees –
For hope would give his limbs the power – and await
A friend that could, he had told her, work his cure
And would be no harsh friend.
                              When night had deepened,
I groped my way from beech to hazel wood,
Found that old house, a sputtering torch within,
And stretched out sleeping on a pile of skins
Ardan, and though I called to him and tried
To shake him out of sleep, I could not rouse him.
I waited till the night was on the turn,
Then fearing that some labourer, on his way
To plough or pasture-land, might see me there,
Went out.
           Among the ivy-covered rocks,
As on the blue light of a sword, a man
Who had unnatural majesty, and eyes
Like the eyes of some great kite scouring the woods,
Stood on my path. Trembling from head to foot
I gazed at him like grouse upon a kite;
But with a voice that had unnatural music,
"A weary wooing and a long," he said,
"Speaking of love through other lips and looking
Under the eyelids of another, for it was my craft
That put a passion in the sleeper there,
And when I had got my will and drawn you here,
Where I may speak to you alone, my craft
Sucked up the passion out of him again
And left mere sleep. He'll wake when the sun wakes,
Push out his vigorous limbs and rub his eyes,
And wonder what has ailed him these twelve months."
I cowered back upon the wall in terror,
But that sweet-sounding voice ran on: "Woman,
I was your husband when you rode the air,
Danced in the whirling foam and in the dust,
In days you have not kept in memory,
Being betrayed into a cradle, and I come

That I may claim you as my wife again."
I was no longer terrified – his voice
Had half awakened some old memory –
Yet answered him, "I am King Eochaid's wife
And with him have found every happiness
Women can find." With a most masterful voice,
That made the body seem as it were a string
Under a bow, he cried, "What happiness
Can lovers have that know their happiness
Must end at the dumb stone? But where we build
Our sudden palaces in the still air
Pleasure itself can bring no weariness,
Nor can time waste the cheek, nor is there foot
That has grown weary of the wandering dance,
Nor an unlaughing mouth, but mine that mourns,
Among those mouths that sing their sweethearts' praise,
Your empty bed." "How should I love," I answered,
"Were it not that when the dawn has lit my bed
And shown my husband sleeping there, I have sighed,
'Your strength and nobleness will pass away'?
Or how should love be worth its pains were it not
That when he has fallen asleep within my arms,
Being wearied out, I love in man the child?
What can they know of love that do not know
She builds her nest upon a narrow ledge
Above a windy precipice?" Then he:
"Seeing that when you come to the deathbed
You must return, whether you would or no,
This human life blotted from memory,
Why must I live some thirty, forty years,
Alone with all this useless happiness?"
Thereon he seized me in his arms, but I
Thrust him away with both my hands and cried,
"Never will I believe there is any change
Can blot out of my memory this life
Sweetened by death, but if I could believe,
That were a double hunger in my lips

For what is doubly brief."
                              And now the shape
My hands were pressed to vanished suddenly.
I staggered, but a beech tree stayed my fall,
And clinging to it I could hear the cocks
Crow upon Tara.'
                    King Eochaid bowed his head
And thanked her for her kindness to his brother,
For that she promised, and for that refused.
Thereon the bellowing of the empounded herds
Rose round the walls, and through the bronze-ringed door
Jostled and shouted those war-wasted men,
And in the midst King Eochaid's brother stood,
And bade all welcome, being ignorant.

A Thought from Propertius

She might, so noble from head
To great shapely knees
The long flowing line,
Have walked to the altar
Through the holy images
At Pallas Athene's side,
Or been fit spoil for a centaur
Drunk with the unmixed wine.

Her Praise

She is foremost of those that I would hear praised.
I have gone about the house, gone up and down
As a man does who has published a new book,
Or a young girl dressed out in her new gown,
And though I have turned the talk by hook or crook
Until her praise should be the uppermost theme,

A woman spoke of some new tale she had read,
A man confusedly in a half dream
As though some other name ran in his head.
She is foremost of those that I would hear praised.
I will talk no more of books or the long war
But walk by the dry thorn until I have found
Some beggar sheltering from the wind, and there
Manage the talk until her name come round.
If there be rags enough he will know her name
And be well pleased remembering it, for in the old days,
Though she had young men's praise and old men's blame,
Among the poor both old and young gave her praise.

His Phoenix

There is a queen in China, or maybe it's in Spain,
And birthdays and holidays such praises can be heard
Of her unblemished lineaments, a whiteness with no stain,
That she might be that sprightly girl trodden by a bird;
And there's a score of duchesses, surpassing womankind,
Or who have found a painter to make them so for pay
And smooth out stain and blemish with the elegance of his mind:
I knew a phoenix in my youth, so let them have their day.

The young men every night applaud their Gaby's laughing eye,
And Ruth St. Denis had more charm although she had poor luck;
From nineteen hundred nine or ten, Pavlova's had the cry,
And there's a player in the States who gathers up her cloak
And flings herself out of the room when Juliet would be bride
With all a woman's passion, a child's imperious way,
And there are – but no matter if there are scores beside:
I knew a phoenix in my youth, so let them have their day.

There's Margaret and Marjorie and Dorothy and Nan,
A Daphne and a Mary who live in privacy;
One's had her fill of lovers, another's had but one,
Another boasts, 'I pick and choose and have but two or three.'
If head and limb have beauty and the instep's high and light
They can spread out what sail they please for all I have to say,
Be but the breakers of men's hearts or engines of delight:
I knew a phoenix in my youth, so let them have their day.

There'll be that crowd, that barbarous crowd, through all the
   centuries,
And who can say but some young belle may walk and talk men wild
Who is my beauty's equal, though that my heart denies,
But not the exact likeness, the simplicity of a child,
And that proud look as though she had gazed into the burning sun,
And all the shapely body no tittle gone astray.
I mourn for that most lonely thing; and yet God's will be done:
I knew a phoenix in my youth, so let them have their day.

A Deep-sworn Vow

Others because you did not keep
That deep-sworn vow have been friends of mine;
Yet always when I look death in the face,
When I clamber to the heights of sleep,
Or when I grow excited with wine,
Suddenly I meet your face.

Broken Dreams

There is grey in your hair.
Young men no longer suddenly catch their breath
When you are passing;
But maybe some old gaffer mutters a blessing

Because it was your prayer
Recovered him upon the bed of death.
For your sole sake – that all heart's ache have known,
And given to others all heart's ache,
From meagre girlhood's putting on
Burdensome beauty – for your sole sake
Heaven has put away the stroke of her doom,
So great her portion in that peace you make
By merely walking in a room.

Your beauty can but leave among us
Vague memories, nothing but memories.
A young man when the old men are done talking
Will say to an old man, 'Tell me of that lady
The poet stubborn with his passion sang us
When age might well have chilled his blood.'

Vague memories, nothing but memories,
But in the grave all, all, shall be renewed.
The certainty that I shall see that lady
Leaning or standing or walking
In the first loveliness of womanhood,
And with the fervour of my youthful eyes,
Has set me muttering like a fool.

You are more beautiful than any one,
And yet your body had a flaw:
Your small hands were not beautiful,
And I am afraid that you will run
And paddle to the wrist
In that mysterious, always brimming lake
Where those that have obeyed the holy law
Paddle and are perfect. Leave unchanged
The hands that I have kissed,
For old sake's sake.

The last stroke of midnight dies.
All day in the one chair
From dream to dream and rhyme to rhyme I have ranged
In rambling talk with an image of air:
Vague memories, nothing but memories.

COMPLEX HARMONIES

The poems in this section were written between 1917 and 1923. They were inspired by Yeats's relationship with his wife Georgie Hyde Lees (George), whom he married in October 1917 and whose automatic writing did much to provide the scaffolding of *A Vision*, which supported poems such as 'Leda and the Swan'.

Owen Aherne and his Dancers

I

A strange thing surely that my Heart, when love had come unsought
Upon the Norman upland or in that poplar shade,
Should find no burden but itself and yet should be worn out.
It could not bear that burden and therefore it went mad.

The south wind brought it longing, and the east wind despair,
The west wind made it pitiful, and the north wind afraid.
It feared to give its love a hurt with all the tempest there;
It feared the hurt that she could give and therefore it went mad.

I can exchange opinion with any neighbouring mind,
I have as healthy flesh and blood as any rhymer's had,
But O! my Heart could bear no more when the upland caught the
    wind;
I ran, I ran, from my love's side because my Heart went mad.

II

The Heart behind its rib laughed out. 'You have called me mad,' it
    said,
'Because I made you turn away and run from that young child;
How could she mate with fifty years that was so wildly bred?
Let the cage bird and the cage bird mate and the wild bird mate in
    the wild.'

'You but imagine lies all day, O murderer,' I replied.
'And all those lies have but one end, poor wretches to betray;
I did not find in any cage the woman at my side.
O but her heart would break to learn my thoughts are far away.'

'Speak all your mind,' my Heart sang out, 'speak all your mind; who
    cares,
Now that your tongue cannot persuade the child till she mistake
Her childish gratitude for love and match your fifty years?
O let her choose a young man now and all for his wild sake.'

Solomon to Sheba

Sang Solomon to Sheba,
And kissed her dusky face,
'All day long from mid-day
We have talked in the one place,
All day long from shadowless noon
We have gone round and round
In the narrow theme of love
Like an old horse in a pound.'

To Solomon sang Sheba,
Planted on his knees,
'If you had broached a matter
That might the learned please,
You had before the sun had thrown
Our shadows on the ground
Discovered that my thoughts, not it,
Are but a narrow pound.'

Said Solomon to Sheba,
And kissed her Arab eyes,
'There's not a man or woman
Born under the skies
Dare match in learning with us two,
And all day long we have found
There's not a thing but love can make
The world a narrow pound.'

Solomon and the Witch

And thus declared that Arab lady:
'Last night, where under the wild moon
On grassy mattress I had laid me,
Within my arms great Solomon,
I suddenly cried out in a strange tongue

Not his, not mine.'
                    Who understood
Whatever has been said, sighed, sung,
Howled, miau-d, barked, brayed, belled, yelled, cried, crowed,
Thereon replied: 'A cockerel
Crew from a blossoming apple bough
Three hundred years before the Fall,
And never crew again till now,
And would not now but that he thought,
Chance being at one with Choice at last,
All that the brigand apple brought
And this foul world were dead at last.
He that crowed out eternity
Thought to have crowed it in again.
For though love has a spider's eye
To find out some appropriate pain –
Aye, though all passion's in the glance –
For every nerve, and tests a lover
With cruelties of Choice and Chance;
And when at last that murder's over
Maybe the bride-bed brings despair,
For each an imagined image brings
And finds a real image there;
Yet the world ends when these two things,
Though several, are a single light,
When oil and wick are burned in one;
Therefore a blessed moon last night
Gave Sheba to her Solomon.'

'Yet the world stays.'
                          'If that be so,
Your cockerel found us in the wrong
Although he thought it worth a crow.
Maybe an image is too strong
Or maybe is not strong enough.'

'The night has fallen; not a sound
In the forbidden sacred grove
Unless a petal hit the ground,
Nor any human sight within it
But the crushed grass where we have lain;
And the moon is wilder every minute.
O! Solomon! let us try again.'

An Image from a Past Life

He. Never until this night have I been stirred.
   The elaborate starlight throws a reflection
   On the dark stream,
   Till all the eddies gleam;
   And thereupon there comes that scream
   From terrified, invisible beast or bird:
   Image of poignant recollection.

She. An image of my heart that is smitten through
   Out of all likelihood, or reason,
   And when at last,
   Youth's bitterness being past,
   I had thought that all my days were cast
   Amid most lovely places; smitten as though
   It had not learned its lesson.

He. Why have you laid your hands upon my eyes?
   What can have suddenly alarmed you
   Whereon 'twere best
   My eyes should never rest?
   What is there but the slowly fading west,
   The river imaging the flashing skies,
   All that to this moment charmed you?

She. A sweetheart from another life floats there
   As though she had been forced to linger
   From vague distress
   Or arrogant loveliness,
   Merely to loosen out a tress
   Among the starry eddies of her hair
   Upon the paleness of a finger.

He. But why should you grow suddenly afraid
   And start – I at your shoulder –
   Imagining
   That any night could bring
   An image up, or anything
   Even to eyes that beauty had driven mad,
   But images to make me fonder?

She. Now she has thrown her arms above her head;
   Whether she threw them up to flout me,
   Or but to find,
   Now that no fingers bind,
   That her hair streams upon the wind,
   I do not know, that know I am afraid
   Of the hovering thing night brought me.

A Prayer for my Daughter

Once more the storm is howling, and half hid
Under this cradle-hood and coverlid
My child sleeps on. There is no obstacle
But Gregory's wood and one bare hill
Whereby the haystack- and roof-levelling wind,
Bred on the Atlantic, can be stayed;
And for an hour I have walked and prayed
Because of the great gloom that is in my mind.

I have walked and prayed for this young child an hour
And heard the sea-wind scream upon the tower,
And under the arches of the bridge, and scream
In the elms above the flooded stream;
Imagining in excited reverie
That the future years had come,
Dancing to a frenzied drum,
Out of the murderous innocence of the sea.

May she be granted beauty and yet not
Beauty to make a stranger's eye distraught,
Or hers before a looking-glass, for such,
Being made beautiful overmuch,
Consider beauty a sufficient end,
Lose natural kindness and maybe
The heart-revealing intimacy
That chooses right, and never find a friend.

Helen being chosen found life flat and dull
And later had much trouble from a fool,
While that great Queen, that rose out of the spray,
Being fatherless could have her way
Yet chose a bandy-leggèd smith for man.
It's certain that fine women eat
A crazy salad with their meat
Whereby the Horn of Plenty is undone.

In courtesy I'd have her chiefly learned;
Hearts are not had as a gift but hearts are earned
By those that are not entirely beautiful;
Yet many, that have played the fool
For beauty's very self, has charm made wise,
And many a poor man that has roved,
Loved and thought himself beloved,
From a glad kindness cannot take his eyes.

May she become a flourishing hidden tree
That all her thoughts may like the linnet be,
And have no business but dispensing round
Their magnanimities of sound,
Nor but in merriment begin a chase,
Nor but in merriment a quarrel.
O may she live like some green laurel
Rooted in one dear perpetual place.

My mind, because the minds that I have loved,
The sort of beauty that I have approved,
Prosper but little, has dried up of late,
Yet knows that to be choked with hate
May well be of all evil chances chief.
If there's no hatred in a mind
Assault and battery of the wind
Can never tear the linnet from the leaf.

An intellectual hatred is the worst,
So let her think opinions are accursed.
Have I not seen the loveliest woman born
Out of the mouth of Plenty's horn,
Because of her opinionated mind
Barter that horn and every good
By quiet natures understood
For an old bellows full of angry wind?

Considering that, all hatred driven hence,
The soul recovers radical innocence
And learns at last that it is self-delighting,
Self-appraising, self-affrighting,
And that its own sweet will is Heaven's will;
She can, though every face should scowl
And every windy quarter howl
Or every bellows burst, be happy still.

And may her bridegroom bring her to a house
Where all's accustomed, ceremonious;
For arrogance and hatred are the wares
Peddled in the thoroughfares.
How but in custom and in ceremony
Are innocence and beauty born?
Ceremony's a name for the rich horn,
And custom for the spreading laurel tree.

The Gift of Harun Al-Rashid

Kusta ben Luka is my name, I write
To Abd Al-Rabban; fellow-roysterer once,
Now the good Caliph's learned Treasurer,
And for no ear but his.
                              Carry this letter
Through the great gallery of the Treasure House
Where banners of the Caliphs hang, night-coloured
But brilliant as the night's embroidery,
And wait war's music; pass the little gallery;
Pass books of learning from Byzantium
Written in gold upon a purple stain,
And pause at last, I was about to say,
At the great book of Sappho's song; but no,
For should you leave my letter there, a boy's
Love-lorn, indifferent hands might come upon it
And let it fall unnoticed to the floor.
Pause at the Treatise of Parmenides
And hide it there, for Caliphs to world's end
Must keep that perfect, as they keep her song,
So great its fame.
                              When fitting time has passed
The parchment will disclose to some learned man
A mystery that else had found no chronicler
But the wild Bedouin. Though I approve

Those wanderers that welcomed in their tents
What great Harun Al-Rashid, occupied
With Persian embassy or Grecian war,
Must needs neglect, I cannot hide the truth
That wandering in a desert, featureless
As air under a wing, can give birds' wit.
In after time they will speak much of me
And speak but fantasy. Recall the year
When our beloved Caliph put to death
His Vizir Jaffer for an unknown reason:
'If but the shirt upon my body knew it
I'd tear it off and throw it in the fire.'
That speech was all that the town knew, but he
Seemed for a while to have grown young again;
Seemed so on purpose, muttered Jaffer's friends,
That none might know that he was conscience-struck –
But that's a traitor's thought. Enough for me
That in the early summer of the year
The mightiest of the princes of the world
Came to the least considered of his courtiers;
Sat down upon the fountain's marble edge,
One hand amid the goldfish in the pool;
And thereupon a colloquy took place
That I commend to all the chroniclers
To show how violent great hearts can lose
Their bitterness and find the honeycomb.

'I have brought a slender bride into the house;
You know the saying, "Change the bride with spring."
And she and I, being sunk in happiness,
Cannot endure to think you tread these paths,
When evening stirs the jasmine bough, and yet
Are brideless.'

                'I am falling into years.'

'But such as you and I do not seem old
Like men who live by habit. Every day
I ride with falcon to the river's edge
Or carry the ringed mail upon my back,
Or court a woman; neither enemy,
Game-bird, nor woman does the same thing twice;
And so a hunter carries in the eye
A mimicry of youth. Can poet's thought
That springs from body and in body falls
Like this pure jet, now lost amid blue sky,
Now bathing lily leaf and fish's scale,
Be mimicry?'
        'What matter if our souls
Are nearer to the surface of the body
Than souls that start no game and turn no rhyme!
The soul's own youth and not the body's youth
Shows through our lineaments. My candle's bright,
My lantern is too loyal not to show
That it was made in your great father's reign.'

'And yet the jasmine season warms our blood.'

'Great prince, forgive the freedom of my speech:
You think that love has seasons, and you think
That if the spring bear off what the spring gave
The heart need suffer no defeat; but I
Who have accepted the Byzantine faith,
That seems unnatural to Arabian minds,
Think when I choose a bride I choose for ever;
And if her eye should not grow bright for mine
Or brighten only for some younger eye,
My heart could never turn from daily ruin,
Nor find a remedy.'
        'But what if I
Have lit upon a woman who so shares
Your thirst for those old crabbed mysteries,
So strains to look beyond our life, an eye
That never knew that strain would scarce seem bright,

And yet herself can seem youth's very fountain,
Being all brimmed with life?'
                              'Were it but true
I would have found the best that life can give,
Companionship in those mysterious things
That make a man's soul or a woman's soul
Itself and not some other soul.'
                              'That love
Must needs be in this life and in what follows
Unchanging and at peace, and it is right
Every philosopher should praise that love.
But I being none can praise its opposite.
It makes my passion stronger but to think
Like passion stirs the peacock and his mate,
The wild stag and the doe; that mouth to mouth
Is a man's mockery of the changeless soul.'

And thereupon his bounty gave what now
Can shake more blossom from autumnal chill
Than all my bursting springtime knew. A girl
Perched in some window of her mother's house
Had watched my daily passage to and fro;
Had heard impossible history of my past;
Imagined some impossible history
Lived at my side; thought time's disfiguring touch
Gave but more reason for a woman's care.
Yet was it love of me, or was it love
Of the stark mystery that has dazed my sight,
Perplexed her fantasy and planned her care?
Or did the torchlight of that mystery
Pick out my features in such light and shade
Two contemplating passions chose one theme
Through sheer bewilderment? She had not paced
The garden paths, nor counted up the rooms,
Before she had spread a book upon her knees
And asked about the pictures or the text;
And often those first days I saw her stare

On old dry writing in a learned tongue,
On old dry faggots that could never please
The extravagance of spring; or move a hand
As if that writing or the figured page
Were some dear cheek.
                              Upon a moonless night
I sat where I could watch her sleeping form,
And wrote by candle-light; but her form moved,
And fearing that my light disturbed her sleep
I rose that I might screen it with a cloth.
I heard her voice, 'Turn that I may expound
What's bowed your shoulder and made pale your cheek';
And saw her sitting upright on the bed;
Or was it she that spoke or some great Djinn?
I say that a Djinn spoke. A livelong hour
She seemed the learned man and I the child;
Truths without father came, truths that no book
Of all the uncounted books that I have read,
Nor thought out of her mind or mine begot,
Self-born, high-born, and solitary truths,
Those terrible implacable straight lines
Drawn through the wandering vegetative dream,
Even those truths that when my bones are dust
Must drive the Arabian host.
                              The voice grew still,
And she lay down upon her bed and slept,
But woke at the first gleam of day, rose up
And swept the house and sang about her work
In childish ignorance of all that passed.
A dozen nights of natural sleep, and then
When the full moon swam to its greatest height
She rose, and with her eyes shut fast in sleep
Walked through the house. Unnoticed and unfelt
I wrapped her in a hooded cloak, and she,
Half running, dropped at the first ridge of the desert
And there marked out those emblems on the sand
That day by day I study and marvel at,

With her white finger. I led her home asleep
And once again she rose and swept the house
In childish ignorance of all that passed.
Even to-day, after some seven years
When maybe thrice in every moon her mouth
Murmured the wisdom of the desert Djinns,
She keeps that ignorance, nor has she now
That first unnatural interest in my books.
It seems enough that I am there; and yet,
Old fellow-student, whose most patient ear
Heard all the anxiety of my passionate youth,
It seems I must buy knowledge with my peace.
What if she lose her ignorance and so
Dream that I love her only for the voice,
That every gift and every word of praise
Is but a payment for that midnight voice
That is to age what milk is to a child?
Were she to lose her love, because she had lost
Her confidence in mine, or even lose
Its first simplicity, love, voice and all,
All my fine feathers would be plucked away
And I left shivering. The voice has drawn
A quality of wisdom from her love's
Particular quality. The signs and shapes;
All those abstractions that you fancied were
From the great Treatise of Parmenides;
All, all those gyres and cubes and midnight things
Are but a new expression of her body
Drunk with the bitter sweetness of her youth.
And now my utmost mystery is out.
A woman's beauty is a storm-tossed banner;
Under it wisdom stands, and I alone –
Of all Arabia's lovers I alone –
Nor dazzled by the embroidery, nor lost
In the confusion of its night-dark folds,
Can hear the armed man speak.

Leda and the Swan

A sudden blow: the great wings beating still
Above the staggering girl, her thighs caressed
By the dark webs, her nape caught in his bill,
He holds her helpless breast upon his breast.

How can those terrified vague fingers push
The feathered glory from her loosening thighs?
And how can body, laid in that white rush,
But feel the strange heart beating where it lies?

A shudder in the loins engenders there
The broken wall, the burning roof and tower
And Agamemnon dead.
       Being so caught up,
So mastered by the brute blood of the air,
Did she put on his knowledge with his power
Before the indifferent beak could let her drop?

FROM 'A WOMAN YOUNG AND OLD'

The poems in this section were written in 1926 and 1927. Yeats described them and the poems of the next section, *A Man Young and Old*, as two series of poems in which a man and a woman in old or later life remember love.

Her Triumph

I did the dragon's will until you came
Because I had fancied love a casual
Improvisation, or a settled game
That followed if I let the kerchief fall:
Those deeds were best that gave the minute wings
And heavenly music if they gave it wit;
And then you stood among the dragon-rings.
I mocked, being crazy, but you mastered it
And broke the chain and set my ankles free,
Saint George or else a pagan Perseus;
And now we stare astonished at the sea,
And a miraculous strange bird shrieks at us.

Consolation

O but there is wisdom
In what the sages said;
But stretch that body for a while
And lay down that head
Till I have told the sages
Where man is comforted.

How could passion run so deep
Had I never thought
That the crime of being born
Blackens all our lot?
But where the crime's committed
The crime can be forgot.

Chosen

The lot of love is chosen. I learnt that much
Struggling for an image on the track
Of the whirling Zodiac.
Scarce did he my body touch,
Scarce sank he from the west
Or found a subterranean rest
On the maternal midnight of my breast
Before I had marked him on his northern way,
And seemed to stand although in bed I lay.

I struggled with the horror of daybreak,
I chose it for my lot! If questioned on
My utmost pleasure with a man
By some new-married bride, I take
That stillness for a theme
Where his heart my heart did seem
And both adrift on the miraculous stream
Where – wrote a learned astrologer –
The Zodiac is changed into a sphere.

Parting

He. Dear, I must be gone
   While night shuts the eyes
   Of the household spies;
   That song announces dawn.

She. No, night's bird and love's
   Bids all true lovers rest,
   While his loud song reproves
   The murderous stealth of day.

He. Daylight already flies
   From mountain crest to crest.

She. That light is from the moon.

He. That bird . . .

She. Let him sing on,
    I offer to love's play
    My dark declivities.

Her Vision in the Wood

Dry timber under that rich foliage,
At wine-dark midnight in the sacred wood,
Too old for a man's love I stood in rage
Imagining men. Imagining that I could
A greater with a lesser pang assuage
Or but to find if withered vein ran blood,
I tore my body that its wine might cover
Whatever could recall the lip of lover.

And after that I held my fingers up,
Stared at the wine-dark nail, or dark that ran
Down every withered finger from the top;
But the dark changed to red, and torches shone,
And deafening music shook the leaves; a troop
Shouldered a litter with a wounded man,
Or smote upon the string and to the sound
Sang of the beast that gave the fatal wound.

All stately women moving to a song
With loosened hair or foreheads grief-distraught,
It seemed a Quattrocento painter's throng,
A thoughtless image of Mantegna's thought –
Why should they think that are for ever young?
Till suddenly in grief's contagion caught,
I stared upon his blood-bedabbled breast
And sang my malediction with the rest.

That thing all blood and mire, that beast-torn wreck,
Half turned and fixed a glazing eye on mine,
And, though love's bitter-sweet had all come back,
Those bodies from a picture or a coin
Nor saw my body fall nor heard it shriek,
Nor knew, drunken with singing as with wine,
That they had brought no fabulous symbol there
But my heart's victim and its torturer.

A Last Confession

What lively lad most pleasured me
Of all that with me lay?
I answer that I gave my soul
And loved in misery,
But had great pleasure with a lad
That I loved bodily.

Flinging from his arms I laughed
To think his passion such
He fancied that I gave a soul
Did but our bodies touch,
And laughed upon his breast to think
Beast gave beast as much.

I gave what other women gave
That stepped out of their clothes,
But when this soul, its body off,
Naked to naked goes,
He it has found shall find therein
What none other knows,

And give his own and take his own
And rule in his own right;
And though it loved in misery
Close and cling so tight,
There's not a bird of day that dare
Extinguish that delight.

FROM 'A MAN YOUNG AND OLD'

The poems in this section were written between 1926 and 1927, a companion series to *A Woman Young and Old*. Yeats called both series contrasting poems of youth.

First Love

Though nurtured like the sailing moon
In beauty's murderous brood,
She walked awhile and blushed awhile
And on my pathway stood
Until I thought her body bore
A heart of flesh and blood.

But since I laid a hand thereon
And found a heart of stone
I have attempted many things
And not a thing is done,
For every hand is lunatic
That travels on the moon.

She smiled and that transfigured me
And left me but a lout,
Maundering here, and maundering there,
Emptier of thought
Than the heavenly circuit of its stars
When the moon sails out.

Human Dignity

Like the moon her kindness is,
If kindness I may call
What has no comprehension in't,
But is the same for all
As though my sorrow were a scene
Upon a painted wall.

So like a bit of stone I lie
Under a broken tree.
I could recover if I shrieked
My heart's agony
To passing bird, but I am dumb
From human dignity.

The Mermaid

A mermaid found a swimming lad,
Picked him for her own,
Pressed her body to his body,
Laughed; and plunging down
Forgot in cruel happiness
That even lovers drown.

The Empty Cup

A crazy man that found a cup,
When all but dead of thirst,
Hardly dared to wet his mouth
Imagining, moon-accursed,
That another mouthful
And his beating heart would burst.
October last I found it too
But found it dry as bone,
And for that reason am I crazed
And my sleep is gone.

His Memories

We should be hidden from their eyes,
Being but holy shows
And bodies broken like a thorn
Whereon the bleak north blows,
To think of buried Hector
And that none living knows.

The women take so little stock
In what I do or say
They'd sooner leave their cosseting
To hear a jackass bray;
My arms are like the twisted thorn
And yet there beauty lay;

The first of all the tribe lay there
And did such pleasure take –
She who had brought great Hector down
And put all Troy to wreck –
That she cried into this ear,
'Strike me if I shriek.'

FROM 'WORDS FOR MUSIC PERHAPS'

The poems in this section were written between 1929 and 1931. Yeats called this group of poems *Words for Music Perhaps* in memory of the exultant weeks when he wrote most of them.

Lullaby

Belovèd, may your sleep be sound
That have found it where you fed.
What were all the world's alarms
To mighty Paris when he found
Sleep upon a golden bed
That first dawn in Helen's arms?

Sleep, belovèd, such a sleep
As did that wild Tristram know
When, the potion's work being done,
Roe could run or doe could leap
Under oak and beechen bough,
Roe could leap or doe could run;

Such a sleep and sound as fell
Upon Eurotas' grassy bank
When the holy bird, that there
Accomplished his predestined will,
From the limbs of Leda sank
But not from her protecting care.

Young Man's Song

'She will change,' I cried,
'Into a withered crone.'
The heart in my side,
That so still had lain,
In noble rage replied
And beat upon the bone;

'Uplift those eyes and throw
Those glances unafraid:
She would as bravely show
Did all the fabric fade;
No withered crone I saw
Before the world was made.'

Abashed by that report,
For the heart cannot lie,
I knelt in the dirt.
And all shall bend the knee
To my offended heart
Until it pardon me.

After Long Silence

Speech after long silence; it is right,
All other lovers being estranged or dead,
Unfriendly lamplight hid under its shade,
The curtains drawn upon unfriendly night,
That we descant and yet again descant
Upon the supreme theme of Art and Song:
Bodily decrepitude is wisdom; young
We loved each other and were ignorant.

Crazy Jane on God

That lover of a night
Came when he would,
Went in the dawning light
Whether I would or no;
Men come, men go;
All things remain in God.

Banners choke the sky;
Men-at-arms tread;
Armoured horses neigh
Where the great battle was
In the narrow pass:
All things remain in God.

Before their eyes a house
That from childhood stood
Uninhabited, ruinous,
Suddenly lit up
From door to top:
All things remain in God.

I had wild Jack for a lover;
Though like a road
That men pass over
My body makes no moan
But sings on:
All things remain in God.

Crazy Jane and Jack the Journeyman

I know, although when looks meet
I tremble to the bone,
The more I leave the door unlatched
The sooner love is gone,
For love is but a skein unwound
Between the dark and dawn.

A lonely ghost the ghost is
That to God shall come;
I – love's skein upon the ground,
My body in the tomb –
Shall leap into the light lost
In my mother's womb.

But were I left to lie alone
In an empty bed,
The skein so bound us ghost to ghost
When he turned his head
Passing on the road that night,
Mine must walk when dead.

Crazy Jane talks with the Bishop

I met the Bishop on the road
And much said he and I.
'Those breasts are flat and fallen now,
Those veins must soon be dry;
Live in a heavenly mansion,
Not in some foul sty.'

'Fair and foul are near of kin,
And fair needs foul,' I cried.
'My friends are gone, but that's a truth
Nor grave nor bed denied,
Learned in bodily lowliness
And in the heart's pride.

'A woman can be proud and stiff
When on love intent;
But Love has pitched his mansion in
The place of excrement;
For nothing can be sole or whole
That has not been rent.'

TESTIMONIES OF LATER YEARS

The poems in this section were written between 1931 and 1938 (less than a year before Yeats died, in January 1939). They pay tribute to Lady Gregory and Maud Gonne, and to a younger friend, Margot Ruddock, and show differing attitudes to the complexities of love.

OK, he said that the bonus question was inspired by the Sopranos, and I lated

Coole and Ballylee, 1931

Under my window-ledge the waters race,
Otters below and moor-hens on the top,
Run for a mile undimmed in Heaven's face
Then darkening through 'dark' Raftery's 'cellar' drop,
Run underground, rise in a rocky place
In Coole demesne, and there to finish up
Spread to a lake and drop into a hole.
What's water but the generated soul?

Upon the border of that lake's a wood
Now all dry sticks under a wintry sun,
And in a copse of beeches there I stood,
For Nature's pulled her tragic buskin on
And all the rant's a mirror of my mood;
At sudden thunder of the mounting swan
I turned about and looked where branches break
The glittering reaches of the flooded lake.

Another emblem there! That stormy white
But seems a concentration of the sky;
And, like the soul, it sails into the sight
And in the morning's gone, no man knows why;
And is so lovely that it sets to right
What knowledge or its lack had set awry,
So arrogantly pure, a child might think
It can be murdered with a spot of ink.

Sound of a stick upon the floor, a sound
From somebody that toils from chair to chair;
Beloved books that famous hands have bound,
Old marble heads, old pictures everywhere;
Great rooms where travelled men and children found
Content or joy; a last inheritor
Where none has reigned that lacked a name and fame
Or out of folly into folly came.

A spot whereon the founders lived and died
Seemed once more dear than life; ancestral trees,
Or gardens rich in memory glorified
Marriages, alliances and families,
And every bride's ambition satisfied.
Where fashion or mere fantasy decrees
We shift about – all that great glory spent –
Like some poor Arab tribesman and his tent.

We were the last romantics – chose for theme
Traditional sanctity and loveliness;
Whatever's written in what poets name
The book of the people; whatever most can bless
The mind of man or elevate a rhyme;
But all is changed, that high horse riderless,
Though mounted in that saddle Homer rode
Where the swan drifts upon a darkening flood.

Quarrel in Old Age

Where had her sweetness gone?
What fanatics invent
In this blind bitter town,
Fantasy or incident
Not worth thinking of,
Put her in a rage.
I had forgiven enough
That had forgiven old age.

All lives that has lived;
So much is certain;
Old sages were not deceived:
Somewhere beyond the curtain
Of distorting days
Lives that lonely thing
That shone before these eyes
Targeted, trod like Spring.

Ribh at the Tomb of Baile and Aillinn

Because you have found me in the pitch-dark night
With open book you ask me what I do.
Mark and digest my tale, carry it afar
To those that never saw this tonsured head
Nor heard this voice that ninety years have cracked.
Of Baile and Aillinn you need not speak,
All know their tale, all know what leaf and twig,
What juncture of the apple and the yew,
Surmount their bones; but speak what none have heard.

The miracle that gave them such a death
Transfigured to pure substance what had once
Been bone and sinew; when such bodies join
There is no touching here, nor touching there,
Nor straining joy, but whole is joined to whole;
For the intercourse of angels is a light
Where for its moment both seem lost, consumed.

Here in the pitch-dark atmosphere above
The trembling of the apple and the yew,
Here on the anniversary of their death,
The anniversary of their first embrace,
Those lovers, purified by tragedy,
Hurry into each other's arms; these eyes,
By water, herb and solitary prayer
Made aquiline, are open to that light.
Though somewhat broken by the leaves, that light
Lies in a circle on the grass; therein
I turn the pages of my holy book.

Margot

All famine struck sat I, and then
Those generous eyes on mine were cast,
Sat like other aged men
Dumfoundered, gazing on a past
That appeared constructed of
Lost opportunities to love.

O how can I that interest hold?
What offer to attentive eyes?
Mind grows young and body old;
When half-closed her eye-lid lies
A sort of hidden glory shall
About these stooping shoulders fall.

The Age of Miracles renew,
Let me be loved as though still young
Or let me fancy that it's true,
When my brief final years are gone
You shall have time to turn away
And cram those open eyes with day.

The Spur

You think it horrible that lust and rage
Should dance attention upon my old age;
They were not such a plague when I was young;
What else have I to spur me into song?

The Three Bushes

An incident from the 'Historia mei Temporis' of the Abbé Michel de Bourdeille.

Said lady once to lover,
'None can rely upon
A love that lacks its proper food;
And if your love were gone
How could you sing those songs of love?
I should be blamed, young man.'
    O my dear, O my dear.

'Have no lit candles in your room,'
That lovely lady said,
'That I at midnight by the clock
May creep into your bed,
For if I saw myself creep in
I think I should drop dead.'
    O my dear, O my dear.

'I love a man in secret,
Dear chambermaid,' said she.
'I know that I must drop down dead
If he stop loving me,
Yet what could I but drop down dead
If I lost my chastity?'
    O my dear, O my dear.

'So you must lie beside him
And let him think me there.
And maybe we are all the same
Where no candles are,
And maybe we are all the same
That strip the body bare.'
    O my dear, O my dear.

But no dogs barked, and midnights chimed,
And through the chime she'd say,
'That was a lucky thought of mine,
My lover looked so gay';
But heaved a sigh if the chambermaid
Looked half asleep all day.
   O my dear, O my dear.

'No, not another song,' said he,
'Because my lady came
A year ago for the first time
At midnight to my room,
And I must lie between the sheets
When the clock begins to chime.'
   O my dear, O my dear.

'A laughing, crying, sacred song,
A leching song,' they said.
Did ever men hear such a song?
No, but that day they did.
Did ever man ride such a race?
No, not until he rode.
   O my dear, O my dear.

But when his horse had put its hoof
Into a rabbit-hole
He dropped upon his head and died.
His lady saw it all
And dropped and died thereon, for she
Loved him with her soul.
   O my dear, O my dear.

The chambermaid lived long, and took
Their graves into her charge,
And there two bushes planted
That when they had grown large
Seemed sprung from but a single root
So did their roses merge.
   O my dear, O my dear.

When she was old and dying,
The priest came where she was;
She made a full confession.
Long looked he in her face,
And O he was a good man
And understood her case.
    O my dear, O my dear.

He bade them take and bury her
Beside her lady's man,
And set a rose-tree on her grave,
And now none living can,
When they have plucked a rose there,
Know where its roots began.
    O my dear, O my dear.

The Lady's First Song

I turn round
Like a dumb beast in a show,
Neither know what I am
Nor where I go,
My language beaten
Into one name;
I am in love
And that is my shame.
What hurts the soul
My soul adores,
No better than a beast
Upon all fours.

A Bronze Head

Here at right of the entrance this bronze head,
Human, superhuman, a bird's round eye,
Everything else withered and mummy-dead.
What great tomb-haunter sweeps the distant sky
(Something may linger there though all else die;)
And finds there nothing to make its terror less
Hysterica passio of its own emptiness?

No dark tomb-haunter once; her form all full
As though with magnanimity of light,
Yet a most gentle woman; who can tell
Which of her forms has shown her substance right?
Or maybe substance can be composite,
Profound McTaggart thought so, and in a breath
A mouthful held the extreme of life and death.

But even at the starting-post, all sleek and new,
I saw the wildness in her and I thought
A vision of terror that it must live through
Had shattered her soul. Propinquity had brought
Imagination to that pitch where it casts out
All that is not itself: I had grown wild
And wandered murmuring everywhere, 'My child, my child!'

Or else I thought her supernatural;
As though a sterner eye looked through her eye
On this foul world in its decline and fall;
On gangling stocks grown great, great stocks run dry,
Ancestral pearls all pitched into a sty,
Heroic reverie mocked by clown and knave,
And wondered what was left for massacre to save.

Politics

*'In our time the destiny of man presents
    its meanings in political terms.'* – THOMAS MANN

How can I, that girl standing there,
My attention fix
On Roman or on Russian
Or on Spanish politics?
Yet here's a travelled man that knows
What he talks about,
And there's a politician
That has read and thought,
And maybe what they say is true
Of war and war's alarms,
But O that I were young again
And held her in my arms!

NOTES

Romantic Idealism

p. 24, *Down by the Salley Gardens*   'Salley gardens' are gardens of
willow used in the thatching of roofs. There was a row of thatched
houses on the bank of the Ballisodare river in County Sligo, and each of
these houses had a salley garden where willows were grown to provide
scollops for the thatch. The poem was an attempt to reconstruct an old
song from three lines imperfectly remembered by an old woman in the
village of Ballisodare. Yeats first gave it the title 'An Old Song Resung'.
It closely resembles a folk song with the same title, a manuscript
version of which is in the P. J. McCall Ballad Collection in the National
Library of Ireland (though two other ballads have been suggested as
sources: 'The Rambling Boys of Pleasure' and 'Going to Mass last
Sunday my True Love passed me by'). Here are the first two stanzas of
the folk song 'Down by the Salley Gardens':

> *Down by the Salley Gardens my own true love and I did meet;*
> *She passed the Salley Gardens, a tripping with her snow white*
>   *feet.*
> *She bid me take life easy just as leaves fall from each tree;*
> *But I being young and foolish with my true love would not*
>   *agree.*
>
> *In a field by the river my lovely girl and I did stand*
> *And leaning on her shoulder I pressed her burning hand,*
> *She bid me take life easy, just as the stream flows o'er the weirs*
> *But I being young and foolish I parted her that day in tears.*

p. 24, *The White Birds*   Yeats wrote this poem to Maud Gonne;
they had been walking on the cliff paths at Howth, the rocky peninsula
which forms the northern arm of Dublin Bay, on the day after he had
first proposed marriage to her and been refused. They were resting
when two seagulls flew overhead on their way out to sea, at which
Maud told him that if she were to have the choice of being any bird she
would prefer'to be a seagull. Three days later he sent her the poem.

The 'Danaan shore' of the third stanza is a reference to the islands
of the fairies; Yeats glossed it as '*Tier-nan-oge*, or fairy-land'. The Irish
words *Tir na nOg* mean the Land of the Young, an afterworld dwelt in
by fairies whose everlasting youth was shared by any mortals who were
brought there, to be forgotten by time. The seagulls are linked with the
birds of fairyland, said, Yeats commented, 'to be as white as snow'. The
poem's general note of weariness is set by the brevity of a meteor tiring
the lovers, while the flames evoke sadness, weariness and fret or worry.
Yeats ties the poem carefully together by repeating words and phrases,
by using alliteration, and by reversing the order of the rose and the lily,
feminine and masculine symbols respectively.

p. 25, *The Sorrow of Love*   Originally written in 1891, this poem
was considerably altered by Yeats in various versions. The girl of the
second stanza is presumably Helen of Troy, though, as the poem is
intended as a tribute to Maud Gonne's beauty, she also symbolises Maud
Gonne. Odysseus had been a suitor of Helen. He married Penelope,
however, and took part in the Greek expedition which besieged Troy to
recover Helen, who married Menelaus, King of Sparta. She had left
Menelaus for Paris, a son of Priam (the last King of Troy, who was
killed by Neoptolemus, the son of Achilles, after the city was taken by
the Greeks); for Paris's winning of Helen, see notes on 'Peace' (p. 122).
Odysseus took nearly ten years to return home to Ithaca after the sack
of Troy; his adventures are the subject of Homer's *Odyssey*.

p. 25, *When You are Old*   This poem was written to Maud Gonne.
It is founded upon 'Quand vous serez bien vieille' by Pierre de Ronsard,
included in his *Sonnets pour Hélène* (1578).

p. 26, *The Rose of the World*   This is a poem, originally entitled 'Rosa Mundi', written to Maud Gonne. The Rose was used by Yeats to convey various symbolic meanings. He described it as a favourite symbol with Irish poets, giving a name to more than one poem in both Gaelic and English, and used to personify Ireland, Rose being the name of a black-haired girl in Irish patriotic poetry who, as the Dark Rosaleen, represented Ireland. Yeats had in mind the 'Dark Rosaleen' of a famous poem by the Irish poet James Clarence Mangan, as well as Aubrey de Vere's line 'The little black rose shall be red at last'. And he alluded to the use of the Rose as a symbol of austerity in Gaelic poetry – the 'Rose of Friday'.

The meanings of the word were multiplied in Yeats's own poetry through his association of it with the symbolism of the Order of the Golden Dawn, an occult society, a Rosicrucian order that he joined in March 1890; in its rituals the four-leafed Rose and the Cross formed a mystic marriage, the Rose having feminine sexual elements, the Cross masculine. The Rose was the flower that bloomed on the sacrifice of the Cross. It symbolised spiritual and eternal beauty, and Yeats associated the Red Rose with love and with Intellectual Beauty. In the poems of his second book, *The Countess Kathleen and Various Legends and Lyrics* (1892) – grouped together in 1895 under the heading *The Rose* – he had found, he believed, the only pathway whereon he could hope to see with his own eyes 'the Eternal Rose of Beauty and Peace'.

In addition to its esoteric meanings in his poetry, the Rose carried suggestions of Irish patriotic hopes and it was, of course, a symbol for Maud Gonne herself, so closely associated with the cause of Irish freedom. In this poem Yeats is identifying her with famous figures of Greek and Irish mythology: Helen of Troy (see notes on 'The Sorrow of Love', p. 106) and Deirdre, the daughter of the storyteller of King Conchubar of Ulster. Both women were beautiful and their beauty wrought havoc. Yeats regards Helen as responsible for the fall of Troy, which the Greeks, pursuing her, besieged for ten years and then sacked. Deirdre was the cause of the deaths of the children of Usna, his sons Naoise, Ainle and Ardan. Isolated under the charge of an old nurse, Lavarcham, as Conchubar's intended queen, she fell in love with one of his Red Branch heroes, Naoise, with whom she ran away to Scotland. They were accompanied by his two brothers. Despite Deirdre's forebodings, Naoise was tricked into returning and he and his brothers were treacherously killed by Conchubar (see notes on 'Baile and Aillinn', p. 117).

The poem originally consisted of the first two stanzas only. Yeats added the third later: it records his worrying over Maud Gonne's tiredness (she is 'Weary and kind') after they had been walking over rough roads in the Dublin mountains. His friend George Russell rightly thought the poem better in its original form.

p. 26, *The Pity of Love*   This poem was written to Maud Gonne.

p. 27, *The Poet pleads with the Elemental Powers*   First published in 1892, this poem was originally entitled 'A Mystical Prayer to the Masters of the Elements, Michael, Gabriel and Raphael', who became 'Finvarra, Feacra and Caolte' in *The Second Book of the Rhymers' Club* (1894).

The identity of the Powers has been differently explained; the original title suggests that the three Masters of the Elements correspond to the great powers of wave, wind and fire of the second stanza. The Immortal Rose is the Rosicrucian symbol (see notes on 'The Rose of the World', p. 107) but may here represent Ideal Beauty. The Seven Lights are the Great Bear's seven stars. The Polar Dragon is the constellation of the Dragon. Yeats commented that the Great Bear and the constellation of the Dragon encircle the Tree of Life, on which 'is here imagined the Rose of the Ideal Beauty growing before it was cast into the world'.

The poem is a love poem about Maud Gonne, whom the Great Powers are to encircle and sing into peace.

p. 27, *The Lover tells of the Rose in his Heart*   Another poem written to Maud Gonne which uses the Rose imagery that linked her and Ireland and Yeats's mystic beliefs. Originally entitled 'The Rose in my Heart' in 1892, it appeared as 'Aedh tells of the Rose in his Heart' in *The Wind Among the Reeds* (1899), Aedh being the Irish god of death, a figure who had appeared in Yeats's stories in *The Secret Rose* (1897).

p. 28, *The Cap and Bells*   A poem of 1893, which Yeats said he had dreamed exactly as he had written it. He had another long dream after it, trying to make out its meaning and whether he was to write it in prose or verse: this is how he annotated it in *The Wind Among the Reeds* (1899):

> The first dream was more a vision than a dream, for it was beautiful and coherent, and gave me the sense of illumination and exaltation that one gets from visions, while the second dream was confused and meaningless. The poem has always meant a great deal to me, though, as is the way with symbolic poems, it has not always meant quite the same thing. Blake would have said 'The authors are in eternity and I am quite sure they can only be questioned in dreams.'

The jester's cap and bells, preferred by the lady to his soul and his heart, may have been associated in Yeats's mind with Aengus, the Irish god of love, ecstasy and poetry, for he later wrote, in 1901, of knowing a man (who might well have been himself) who was trying to bring into his mind's eye an image of Aengus 'who changed four of his kisses into birds' and 'suddenly the image of a man with cap and bells rushed before his mind's eye, and grew vivid and spoke and called itself "Aengus' Messenger"'. Yeats regarded this poem as the way to win a lady, 'He wishes for the Cloths of Heaven' (p. 36) as the way to lose one.

p. 29, *Red Hanrahan's Song about Ireland*   This poem first appeared in the *National Observer* in August 1894; it was untitled and part of a story, 'Kathleen the Daughter of Hoolihan and Hanrahan the Red'. In it Hanrahan is linked with places in County Sligo. The present title was first used in 1906. Yeats toughened up the first published version considerably in his rewriting, but the first version with its alliteration and echoing vowels, its assonance and consonance, has a magic of its own:

> *Veering, fleeting, fickle, the winds of Knocknarea,*
> *When in ragged vapour they mutter night and day,*
> *Veering, fleeting, fickle, our loves and angers meet:*
> *But we bend together and kiss the quiet feet*
> *Of Kathleen-ny-Hoolihan.*

Weak and worn and weary the waves of Cummen Strand,
When the wind comes blowing across the hilly land;
Weak and worn and weary our courage droops and dies
But our hearts are lighted from the flame in the eyes
Of Kathleen-ny-Hoolihan.

Dark and dull and earthy the stream of Drumahair
When the wind is pelting out of the wintry air;
Dark and dull and earthy our souls and bodies be:
But pure as a tall candle before the Trinity
Our Kathleen-ny-Hoolihan.

The poem was possibly suggested by James Clarence Mangan's 'Kathleen-ny-Hoolihan'. Kathleen symbolised Ireland in Irish traditions, and Maud Gonne played the part of Cathleen in Yeats's play *Cathleen ni Houlihan* in Dublin in 1902. Hanrahan – Yeats got the name, or part of it, from a shop front in a Galway village – is a hedge schoolmaster and wandering poet. Yeats substituted his name for that of O'Sullivan the Red, or O'Sullivan Rua, used in earlier poems, an invented character based upon an eighteenth-century Irish poet, Eoghan Ruadh O'Suilleabhan (1748–84). His adventures are told in *The Secret Rose* (1897); he is amorous, drunken, a practiser of magic and a mystical patriot, rejected by priests and fairies alike.

p. 30, *He bids his Beloved be at Peace*   Originally entitled 'Michael Robartes bids his Beloved be at Peace', the poem was written to Olivia Shakespear in September 1895. Michael Robartes was a character invented by Yeats, a visionary and a magician, who appeared in 'Rosa Alchemica', one of the stories in *The Secret Rose* (1897) and elsewhere in Yeats's writings.

p. 30, *He gives his Beloved certain Rhymes*   A poem written in 1895, this first appeared in 'The Binding of the Hair', a story published in *The Savoy* in 1896. The 'He' of the title was Aedh (see notes on 'The Lover tells of the Rose in His Heart', p. 108) in *The Wind Among the Reeds* (1899). The story was based on 'some old Gaelic legend', Yeats commented, in which a man 'swears to sing the praise of a certain woman, his head is cut off and the head sings'. The poem is the song sung by the severed head. Joseph Hone, in *W. B. Yeats 1865-1939*, suggested the poem was written to Olivia Shakespear; it was, however, more probably written to Maud Gonne.

p. 31, *He tells of the Perfect Beauty*   A poem written in 1895, this was originally entitled 'O'Sullivan the Red to Mary Lavelle I'. For the invented character O'Sullivan, see notes on 'Red Hanrahan's Song about Ireland' (p. 109); Mary Lavelle appears in the story 'Red Hanrahan' in Yeats's *The Secret Rose* (1897).

p. 31, *A Poet to his Beloved*   This poem, written in 1895, was first entitled 'O'Sullivan the Red to Mary Lavelle II'. For these two invented characters, see notes on 'Red Hanrahan's Song about Ireland' (p. 110) and 'He tells of the Perfect Beauty' (above).

p. 31, *He remembers Forgotten Beauty*   This poem was first entitled 'O'Sullivan Rua to Mary Lavelle' in 1896; this became 'Michael Robartes remembers Forgotten Beauty' in 1899. For O'Sullivan Rua, O'Sullivan the Red in other titles, see notes on 'Red Hanrahan's Song about Ireland' (p. 109); for Mary Lavelle, see notes on 'He tells of the Perfect Beauty' (above). In the story 'Red Hanrahan' (in *The Secret Rose* (1897)) Hanrahan is bewitched after receiving a message from Mary Lavelle that he should go to her, and within a month, or the land would be given to someone else; 'brought away by them', he returns after a year to find her house a ruin and hear that she has married a labouring man and gone with him to look for work in England. He never hears of her again.

p. 32, *The Secret Rose*   Originally entitled 'O'Sullivan Rua to the Secret Rose' this poem first appeared in September 1896. For O'Sullivan Rua, or O'Sullivan the Red, see notes on 'Red Hanrahan's Song about Ireland' (p. 109). Another love poem to Maud Gonne, 'The Secret Rose' blends Christian and pagan imagery with occult, and expresses some of the apocalyptic ideas current towards the end of the nineteenth century, when, as the poem puts it, the stars will be blown about the sky and die 'Like the sparks blown out of a smithy'. The Rose with its great leaves is the Rosicrucian symbol, though it can also suggest Ireland and Maud Gonne (see notes on 'The Rose of the World', p. 107). The Holy Sepulchre of Christian tradition is balanced against a hint of Dionysian rites in the reference to the wine vat. The Rose enfolds the Magi, the three Wise Men, as well as the pagan Irish King of Ulster, Conchubar, who, in this poem, sees the crucifixion of Christ in a vision. The 'vain frenzy' refers to the story told by Geoffrey Keating in his *History of Ireland*, completed in 1634; in it Conchubar asked his druids what had caused the eclipse of sun and moon which occurred on the Friday on which Christ was crucified, and was told by them of Christ's being crucified by the Jews. He said that if he were in Christ's presence he would kill those who were putting him to death. He rushed at a woody grove and began to cut and fell it in an excess of fury. This prompted a ball (made out of the brain of a dead enemy which had lodged in Conchubar's head in battle) to start out of his head, taking some of his own brain with it, which caused his death.

The Irish hero Cuchulain met Fand, the wife of Manannan Mac Lir, god of the sea, by the seashore, after he had been in the Country of the Gods. (Cuchulain had experienced a magical weakness for a year, and was told by Aengus, the god of love, that Fand and her sister Laban would heal his weakness if he came to the Country of the Gods, where he was Fand's lover for a month.) Yeats's notes tell how Cuchulain promised Fand that he would meet her at a place called The Yew at the Strand's End, and returned to earth. There his wife Emer won his love again and Manannan Mac Lir came to The Yew at the Strand's End and brought Fand back to the Country of the Gods. Cuchulain's love for her returned; he went mad when he saw her going away and wandered among the mountains until he was cured by a druid drink of forgetfulness.

The man who drove the gods out of their liss (*lios*, an Irish word for a fort) was the warrior Caoilte, who, when almost all his companions had been killed, after the Battle of Gabhra, attacked the gods and drove them out of their fort, which was either at Ossory or Assaroe.

The 'proud dreaming king' was Fergus MacRoigh, Conchubar's stepfather and predecessor on the Ulster throne; he gave up the kingship to Conchubar; his life in the woods is the subject of Yeats's poem 'Fergus and the Druid'.

The man who sold his property came from 'The Red Pony', a folk tale in William Larminie's *West Irish Folk Tales and Romances* (1893), in which a young man, who found a box on the road with a lock of hair in it, which gave out a light, is employed by a king, who tells him to search for the woman to whom the hair belongs. Eventually it is the young man, not the king, who marries the woman. The woman 'of so shining loveliness' suggests Maud Gonne's beauty.

p. 33, *He reproves the Curlew*   This poem was first published in November 1896 with the title 'Windlestraws I. O'Sullivan Rua to the Curlew'; it became 'Hanrahan reproves the Curlew' in *The Wind Among the Reeds* (1899). For these invented characters see notes on 'Hanrahan's Song about Ireland' (p. 109). The wind is a symbol of vague desires and hopes, the west the region of 'fading and dreaming things'. The poem may have been written to Olivia Shakespear.

p. 33, *He mourns for the Change that has come upon him and his Beloved, and longs for the End of the World*   The opening lines in this poem are closely related to imagery in *The Wanderings of Oisin* (1889). The white deer and the hound with one red ear, Yeats commented in *The Wind Among the Reeds* (1899), were related to the deer and hound that flicker in and out of the various tellings of the Arthurian legends, leading knights on various adventures. He also related them to the hounds and hornless deer at the beginning of tales of Oisin's journey to the Country of the Young. His own source was a Gaelic poem about that journey, probably Michael Comyn's eighteenth-century *The Lay of Oisin in the Land of Youth*, translated by Brian O'Looney, *Transactions of the Ossianic Society* (1859). The hunting of the hornless deer led Oisin to the seashore; there Niamh, the fairy princess, came to seek him; they rode over the sea on her magic horse and on the journey he saw a young man following a girl with a golden apple and afterwards a hound with one ear following a deer with no horns. The hound and the deer seemed to Yeats plain images of the desire of the man for the woman and the desire of the woman 'which is for the desire of the man'.

The 'man with a hazel wand' is Aengus, the Irish god of love. The 'Boar without bristles', Yeats commented, is a symbol of the darkness that will destroy the world. He was aware of Irish prophecies or visions of a great battle to be fought in 'the Valley of the Black Pig', in which Ireland's enemies would be destroyed; he had seen an old man at Lissadell, in County Sligo, fall to the ground as he raved out a description of the battle. Yeats had also discussed the battle with a Sligo countrywoman who thought it would be fought between Ireland and England. He himself associated it with some Armageddon which would 'quench all things in darkness again'.

In the Irish legend the boar that killed Diarmuid at the western end of Ben Bulben in County Sligo was bristleless, and the Boar in this poem will come from the west, probably because Yeats associated it with Sligo and thought the west was linked with dreaming and fading things. He wrote a long note linking Irish peasants' beliefs about the battle and the mysterious Black Pig with material he read in Sir James Frazer and Sir John Rhys, mentioning the boars that killed Adonis and Attis, arguing that the Black Pig was a 'type of cold and winter' and therefore a symbol of the darkness which would destroy the world.

p. 34, *The Song of Wandering Aengus*   This poem, which is largely about Maud Gonne, was suggested to Yeats by a Greek folk song; this was Lucy Garnett's 'The Three Fishes', in *Greek Folk Poetry* (1896). Colonel Russell K. Alspach, who identified this source, thought that 'The White Trout' by Samuel Lover might also have influenced Yeats, who considered Greek and Irish folk beliefs were very similar, and said that when he wrote the poem he was thinking of Ireland and of the spirits that are in Ireland.

The Aengus of the poem's title was the Irish god of youth, beauty and poetry, elsewhere described by Yeats as 'the Master of Love'. Whether Aengus or the poet speaks through the poem is unclear. Aengus is perhaps the persona of the first stanza, for, as Sheila O'Sullivan has suggested, in Standish O'Grady's edition of the story of Diarmuid and Grainne (in the *Translations of the Ossianic Society*, III), Aengus, in the guise of a youth, meets the lovers fleeing from Grainne's husband, Finn, and provides them with food by going into a wood where he plucks a long branch from a quicken tree as a rod, puts a holly berry on a hook as bait and catches them a trout. The 'glimmering girl/With apple blossom in her hair' is an image of Maud Gonne, whom Yeats associated with apple blossom; in *Autobiographies* he described her at their first meeting, in January 1889, as having a luminous complexion 'like that of apple blossom through which the light falls'. In his unpublished autobiography he remembered her 'standing that first day by a great heap of such blossoms [apple blossom was unlikely in January] in the window'. She 'passed before a window and rearranged a spray of flowers in a vase'. Twelve years after 'I put this impression into verse ("she pulled down the pale blossom")'.

The poem's lines ran 'Blossom pale, she pulled down the pale blossom/At the moth hour and hid it in her bosom'. The imagery of 'The silver apples of the moon,/The golden apples of the sun' may derive, Sheila O'Sullivan suggests, from descriptions given by Lady Wilde, Oscar's mother, in her *Ancient Cures, Charms and Usages* (1890) of May Day festivals in which two balls representing sun and moon, covered in gold and silver paper respectively, were suspended within a hoop wreathed with marsh marigold and rowan, and carried in May Day processions in Ireland. The imagery recurred in a poem 'The Man who dreamed of Faeryland'.

p. 35, *He thinks of his Past Greatness when a Part of the Constellations of Heaven*   This poem was originally entitled 'Song of Mongan' in 1898; it then became 'Mongan thinks of his Past Greatness' in 1899. Yeats explained in a note that in old Celtic poetry Mongan was a king and wizard who remembered his past lives. The Country of the Young (Irish *Tir na nOg*) is the land of the gods and the happy dead. The hazel-tree was the Tree of Life or of Knowledge, and in Ireland, Yeats commented, 'it was doubtless as elsewhere the tree of the Heavens'. The Pilot Star is Irish for the Pole Star, the Crooked Plough Irish for the Plough.

p. 35, *He hears the Cry of the Sedge*   This poem was written to Maud Gonne and first appeared in the *Dome* in May 1898, entitled 'Aodh to Dectora/Three Songs/I'; this title was altered to 'Aedh hears the Cry of the Sedge'. (For Aedh, see notes on 'The Lover tells of the Rose in his Heart, p. 108.) The lake may be Coole Lake. In 1897 Yeats spent the first of many summers at Coole Park, Lady Gregory's house in County Galway. He went there exhausted by his campaigning as chairman of the Executive Committee of the Centenary Association, formed to mark the centenary of the Revolution of 1798 and the death of Wolfe Tone, and by the effect of the riots in Dublin against the celebration of Queen Victoria's Diamond Jubilee. He was frustrated in his attempts to write his novel, *The Speckled Bird*, and, of course, he was deeply troubled by his abandonment of his affair with Olivia Shakespear and the resumption of his hopeless passion for Maud Gonne. It would have been a relief, he wrote later, to have screamed aloud as he walked in the woods at Coole; and when desire became an unendurable torture, 'I would masturbate and that, no matter how moderate I was, would make me ill'.

p. 36, *He wishes for the Cloths of Heaven*   After writing this poem, originally entitled 'Aedh wishes for the Cloths of Heaven' (see notes on 'The Lover tells of the Rose in his Heart', p. 108), Yeats described it as the way to lose a lady; by then, of course, he had moved out of writing in a defeatist Pre-Raphaelite way. This very delicate and beautiful poem has, however, its strong note of realism in the line 'But I, being poor, have only my dreams . . .'.

p. 36, *The Harp of Aengus*   This poem, first published in 1900, was placed after the '[Introductory Lines]' to *The Shadowy Waters* in *Poems 1899-1905*. Yeats had read the stories of Aengus and Edain in what he called poor translations. Edain (in some versions of the legend Etain or Adene) went away to live among the Sidhe (Shee, or fairies); she was lured by Midir or Midhir, a King of the Sidhe. 'The Two Kings' (p. 53) tells the story of his wooing. In the Irish tale Aengus, god of love, is a foster-son of Midhir for whom he obtains Edain as a wife. She is turned into a purple fly by Fuamnach, Midhir's previous wife, and, blown by the wind, finds refuge with Aengus in the Boyne Valley; he keeps her in a house of glass, where Yeats imagines her weaving harp-strings out of his hair. (Fuamnach, discovering her whereabouts, used druid spells to call up another wind before being killed by Aengus; the wind, however, blew Edain through Ireland for seven years before Etar drank her down in a glass of wine and bore her as a reincarnated Edain.)

p. 37, *Baile and Aillinn*   This 'half lyrical half narrative' poem was written during July and August 1901. Here is Yeats's note on it of July 1902:

> It is better, I think, to explain at once some of the allusions to mythological people and things, instead of breaking up the reader's attention with a series of foot-notes. What the 'long wars for the White Horn and the Brown Bull' were, and who 'Deirdre the harper's daughter' was, and why Cuchullain [Yeats spelt the hero's name in various ways; the pronunciation is correctly Koohullin or Cu-hullin] was called 'the hound of Ulad', I shall not explain. The reader will find all that he need know about them, and about the story of Baile and Aillinn itself, in Lady Gregory's 'Cuchullain of Muirthemne', the most important book that has come out of Ireland in my time. 'The Great Plain' is the Land of the Dead and of the Happy; it is called also 'The Land of the Living Heart', and many beautiful names besides. And Findrias and Falias and Gorias and Murias were the four mysterious cities whence the Tuatha De Danaan, the divine race, came to Ireland, cities of learning out of sight of the world, where they found their four talismans, the spear, the stone, the cauldron, and the sword. The birds that flutter over the head of Aengus are four birds that he made out of his kisses; and when Baile and Aillinn take the shape of swans linked with a golden chain, they take the shape that other enchanted lovers took before them in the old stories. Midhir was a king of the Sidhe, or people of faery, and Etain his wife, when driven away by a jealous woman, took refuge once upon a time with Aengus in a house of glass, and there I have imagined her weaving harp-strings into 'The Shadowy Waters', where I interpret the myth in my own way.

The long wars were those described in the *Tain Bo Cualgne*. For Deirdre, see below. Cuchulain, originally called Setanta, killed the hound of the smith Culann in self-defence, and after he offered to take its place he was called the Hound of Culann, Cuchulain. For Aengus see notes on 'The Harp of Aengus' (p. 116). Baile was the son of Buan, an Ulster goddess, the wife of Mesgedra, King of Leinster. Aillinn was the daughter of Lugaidh; he was the son of Curoi MacDaire, a Munster king who refrained from attacking Cuchulain when he saw the hero had been wounded in his fight with Ferdiad at the Yellow Ford. The White Horn and the Brown Bull are part of the story of the *Tain Bo Cualgne*, the cattle raid of Cooley made by Maeve, Queen of Connaught, who wanted to obtain the Brown Bull from the north-eastern peninsula of Cooley in Ulster. She was angry that Ailell, her husband, had a white-horned bull better than any animal in her herds.

Muirthemne was a plain in County Louth, called after Muirthemne, son of Breogan, a Milesian leader. Cuchulain had his small kingdom there; it was the site of the main battle of the *Tain Bo Cualgne*. The first 'there' is Rosnaree on the River Boyne, where Baile and Aillinn were to be married. The second 'there', where the old man (the god Aengus in disguise) is running, is Dundalk.

Kate or Nan are names for common lovers. The Hound of Ulad, or Ulster, is another name for Cuchulain. Though he is helping to bury Baile, he is weeping for the earlier fate of the lovers Deirdre, daughter of the bard Felimid, and Naoise, son of Usna ('her man' in the following refrain); they were betrayed unwittingly by Fergus, their safe conduct, when they returned to Ireland from Scotland. Fergus left them alone when invited by Barach to a feast. (He was laid under *geasa* (a kind of tabu) never to refuse an invitation.) This had been arranged by Conchubar (the King of Ulster, the stepson of Fergus, who had previously been King but handed over power to Conchubar. The name can be pronounced as Connahur or Connkubar), who had Naoise and his brothers killed. Deirdre committed suicide later.

Ogham was an ancient Irish script dating to the third century; it had an alphabet of twenty characters and is usually found in stone inscriptions, the characters represented by a straight line with shorter straight lines at right-angles to it. Baile was of the race of Rury or Rudraige, descendants of Fergus MacRoigh. The Great Plain, glossed by Yeats as the Land of the Dead and of the Happy and the Land of the Living Heart, is the central plain of Ireland. The names indicate the home of the gods beneath the River Boyne, which is in the northern part of the plain. The Hill Seat of Laighen is a hill fort, the seat of the Leinster kings, near Kilcullen on the borders of County Dublin and County Kildare. The two swans are the lovers Baile and Aillinn. For Edain, see notes on 'The Harp of Aengus' (p. 116).

The four cities Gorias, Findrias, Falias and Murias have as talismans the Spear which is Lugh's spear; the stone which is the *Lia Fail*, or Stone of Destiny, was brought to Scotland by fifth-century Irish invaders, moved to England by Edward I, called the Stone of Scone and kept in Westminster Abbey. (It was removed by Scottish Nationalists in 1950 and was in Scotland for some time before it was brought back to Westminster Abbey; it is sometimes known as the Coronation Stone.) The cauldron was the Dagda's (he was the chief god of the Tuatha de Danaan) and the sword was Lugh's (he was the sun god and benign). 'The apples of the sun and moon' appear in 'The Song of Wandering Aengus' (p. 34; see note on poem, p. 114), and in another early poem, 'The Man who dreamed of Faeryland'. The fighting at the ford is the fight between Cuchulain and his friend Ferdiad, told in the *Tain Bo Cualgne*. The 'Beloved' is Maud Gonne.

Romantic Realism

p. 46, *The Arrow*   A poem, written in 1901, which goes back to Yeats's first meeting with Maud Gonne in January 1889, with which he associated apple blossom ('The Song of Wandering Aengus', p. 34, uses the same imagery). The arrow may derive from Blake's symbolism in his preface to *Milton*:

> *Bring me my Bow of burning gold:*
> *Bring me my Arrows of desire:*
> *Bring me my Spear: O clouds unfold!*
> *Bring me my Chariot of fire.*

In their three-volume edition of *The Works of William Blake* (1893), Yeats and Edwin Ellis glossed these lines as follows: 'He shall return again, aided by the bow, sexual symbolism, the arrow, desire, the spear, male potency, the chariot, joy.'

p. 46, *Adam's Curse*   This poem, written to Maud Gonne in 1901, arose out of an evening he spent with her and her sister, Mrs Kathleen Pilcher. Maud described the meeting in *A Servant of the Queen* (1938):

> Kathleen and I sat together on a big sofa amid piles of soft cushions. I was still in my dark clothes with the black veil I always wore when travelling instead of a hat, and we must have made a strange contrast. I saw Willie Yeats looking critically at me and he told Kathleen he liked her dress and that she was looking younger than ever. It was on that occasion Kathleen remarked that it was hard work being beautiful which Willie turned into his poem 'Adam's Curse'.

'That beautiful mild woman' was Mrs Pilcher, whom Maud described that evening as 'looking more than ever like a tall lily, with her pale gold hair and white evening dress'. This poem proclaims the need for poetry to seem nonchalant, as if it were spontaneous, despite all the work that goes into its making: something Corinna Salvadori compared in *Yeats and Castiglione* (1965) to the quality of *sprezzatura* so valued and praised by Castiglione in *The Courtier*, a book Yeats admired and knew in the Elizabethan translation by Sir Thomas Hoby and that of 1902 by Opdycke.

p. 47, *The Folly of Being Comforted*   This poem, first published in 1902, records the effect of time. Though Maud Gonne possesses all her great nobleness, the wild summer is no longer in her gaze; he has been told (possibly by Lady Gregory, who, in 1898 when she first met Maud Gonne, who had been ill, saw, instead of the vision of beauty she expected, 'a death's head') that Maud's hair is greying, there are shadows about her eyes. Time, however, will not make things better, replies the poet: there is no comfort in that thought; her beauty is remade by Time.

p. 48, [*Unpublished Lines, written after Maud Gonne married John MacBride*]   Yeats wrote these lines in a diary.

p. 48, *Never Give all the Heart*   Another poem about Yeats's hopeless passion – 'deaf and dumb and blind with love' – for Maud Gonne to whom he 'gave all his heart and lost'; it was written after her marriage to John MacBride in 1903 and first published in 1905. It has affinities with a poem by Blake, 'Love's Secret', which contains the same advice and records the same result.

> *Never seek to tell thy love*
> *Love that never told can be;*
> *For the gentle wind doth move*
> *Silently, invisibly.*
>
> *I told my love, I told my love,*
> *I told her all my heart,*
> *Trembling, cold, in ghastly fears –*
> *Ah, she doth depart!*

p. 48, *No Second Troy*   This poem, one of several grouped under the title 'Raymond Lully and his wife Pernella' (Lully, a Spanish theologian and philosopher, was altered to Nicholas Flamel, an erratum slip in *The Green Helmet* (1910) attributing the mistake to a slip of the pen), was written in December 1908. The use of the astrologer Nicholas Flamel and his wife Pernella harks back to the early 1890s when Maud Gonne was initiated into the Order of the Golden Dawn and Yeats hoped that they would both devote their lives to the pursuit of mystic truth. It suits the mood of these poems which record his passion in the past tense, measuring the waste of spirit his vain love for Maud has involved, but also stating (as in the prose of his unpublished autobiography and the poem 'Words') that she never did or could understand the plans and ideas that underpinned his life, affirming that his best work had been and was being written out of his desire to explain himself to her.

The mention of the astrologer and his wife in the title also hinted at the 'mystic marriage' of 1898 between Yeats and Maud Gonne, renewed in 1908.

This poem is, of course, about Maud Gonne, the 'her' of the first line. She *had* filled his days with misery, particularly through her marriage to John MacBride in 1903; the fact that her marriage broke up in 1905 when she sought a divorce from MacBride in the French courts (and was awarded a separation instead, because MacBride was, unlike her, officially resident in Ireland, not France) caused her to give up public political life (when she appeared with Yeats at the Abbey Theatre in 1906 she was hissed) until about 1918. This inactivity – she was living in France and spent some of her time studying art; she illustrated several books later – is dealt with by the phrase 'of late'. Before the divorce case she had, of course, been deeply involved in anti-British activity. The reference to her teaching 'ignorant men most violent ways' may allude to her plans to incite tenants in Ireland to violence, something from which Yeats (prompted by Lady Gregory) dissuaded her in 1898. The hurling of 'the little streets against the great' may possibly refer to her speeches at the time of the 1897 Jubilee Riots.

The image of the 'tightened bow' may come from Blake (see notes on 'The Arrow', p. 119). Maud's stature, her beauty made her seem as if she lived in some other civilisation; here she is compared to Helen of

Troy (possibly with an echo of Dryden's *Alexander's Feast*: 'And like another *Helen*, fired another Troy'; see also notes on 'The Sorrow of Love', p. 106). Elsewhere she was seen as a classical impersonation of the spring; Virgil's phrase 'she walks like a goddess' seemed 'made for her alone'.

p. 49, *Peace*   This is another poem in the Nicholas Flamel and his wife Pernella grouping (see notes on 'No Second Troy', p. 121), written in May 1910 at Maud Gonne's house, Les Mouettes, at Colleville in Calvados, Normandy. It is tightly held together by alliteration, rhyme and repetition. The Homeric imagery reaches back to 'The Rose of the World' (p. 26). Helen was the wage of the Trojan hero Paris for his role in judging between the three goddesses Aphrodite, Athene and Hera, and awarding Aphrodite the apple (though it could be argued that Helen's husband Menelaus, the Greek hero, got her back as his wage for playing his part in the Greek victory over the Trojans; see notes on 'The Sorrow of Love', p. 106). It is perhaps unlikely that Yeats is regarding too closely the parallel between Helen being Paris's wage and Maud Gonne John MacBride's. MacBride was a soldier, whom Maud regarded as a hero because he had fought for the Boers in the South African war. There may be a suggestion of age-old links between beautiful women and warriors; later, in 'A Prayer for My Daughter' (p. 68), Yeats referred to Aphrodite's choice of Hephaestos, the 'bandy-leggèd smith'. This poem, however, concentrates on Maud's beauty and the contradictions Yeats observed in her character.

p. 49, *Against Unworthy Praise*   Another poem in the Nicholas Flamel and his wife Pernella grouping (see notes on 'No Second Troy', p. 121), this was written in May 1910. The knave and dolt may refer to those members of audiences at the Abbey Theatre who sought to prevent the staging of plays (such as John Millington Synge's *The Playboy of the Western World*, greeted with rioting when it was played in 1907) of which they disapproved (on nationalist grounds, thinking that the image of Ireland presented was unfavourable); the work is not for their praise but has been created for Maud Gonne's sake. Yeats wrote in his diary about this time: 'How much of the best that I have done and still do is but the attempt to explain myself to her'. 'The labyrinth of her days' expresses a feeling he experienced when contemplating Maud's complexity of character; he used the word again in 'The Tower II'. The slander (some of this stemmed from her political opponents, among them Macarthy Teeling, and Frank Hugh O'Donnell whom she and Yeats called 'the mad rogue'; he had issued a pamphlet earlier against Yeats's play *The Countess Cathleen*) and ingratitude shown to her prompted a poem of 1898: 'He thinks of those who have Spoken Evil of his Beloved'; the 'worse wrong' may refer to some of the audience in the Abbey hissing Maud Gonne in 1906 (see notes on 'No Second Troy', p. 121).

p. 50, *Brown Penny*   This poem was first entitled 'Momentary Thoughts/The Young Man's Song' and appeared in *The Green Helmet* (1910). Some of its lines were later rewritten.

p. 51, *Friends*   This poem was written in 1911. It deals with three women with whom Yeats maintained relationships over long periods in his life. The first is Olivia Shakespear, whom he first met at a dinner in 1894. They corresponded frequently when he was in Sligo during 1895. She sent him the manuscript of her novel, *Beauty's Hour*, for criticism; he wrote to her about his views of the coincidence of opposites. They exchanged thoughts freely: nothing came between 'Mind and delighted mind'. Their affair gave Yeats his first experience of sex. Begun in 1896, it 'lasted but a year' and probably ended in February 1897 (hence the reference in the poem to fifteen years); 'the breaking between us', he wrote in his unpublished autobiography, 'for many years'. (He cancelled 'it was the end of our liaison', presumably because sometime after Maud Gonne's marriage in 1903 they began another affair, probably, as Deirdre Toomey has suggested, in 1910.) After Olivia Shakespear's death in 1938 he recorded in a letter how she had been the centre of his life in London and during all that time they had never had a quarrel, 'sadness sometimes, but never a difference'.

There has been comment upon the identification of the second figure, whose

> *hand*
> *Had strength that could unbind*
> *What none can understand,*
> *What none can have and thrive,*
> *Youth's dreamy load, till she*
> *So changed me that I live*
> *Labouring in ecstasy.*

Both Mrs Yeats and Maud Gonne told me that these lines referred to Lady Gregory; Mrs Yeats, who had discussed the poem with her husband, thought that Lady Gregory had freed the way for Yeats to create the Irish theatre of which he had dreamed but almost given up hope of achieving.

In his first long stay in Coole in 1897 he was lost in a mass of images, on the path of the Chameleon, ill in body and soul. In 'The Stirring of the Bones', *Autobiographies* (p. 377) he recorded his debt to Lady Gregory:

> When I was in good health again I found myself indolent partly because I was affrighted by that impossible novel *The Speckled Bird*, and asked her to send me to my work every day at eleven, and at some other hour to my letters, rating me with idleness if need be, and I doubt if I should have done much with my life but for her firmness and her care.

Lady Gregory wanted to be involved in the Irish literary movement; she revived Yeats's interest in folklore, taking him with her to various cottages, collecting material, some of which he used later in a series of articles. She gave him an insight into a more ordered life at a more dignified level than he had known before. In a letter of 1911 he quoted a draft of these lines; the 'dreamy load' was then 'Youth's bitter burden': the poverty and insecurity of which he had told her in July 1897. Because 'dreamy load' has been taken to mean 'a powerfully explicit image for an incapacitating virginity' (which is in any case arguable), it is suggested that, in rewriting, Yeats moved from 'bitter burden' to 'dreamy load', from Lady Gregory's practical aid in ridding him of the burden to a praise of the hand that had strength to unbind the dreamy load of his virginity; but there were many other things besides his virginity, lost in 1896, that occupied his dreaming. Such an interpretation does not necessarily alter the fact that Yeats was primarily praising

Lady Gregory. Maud Gonne, incidentally, told me that she thought that 'Labouring in ecstasy' referred to the effect of the Italian tour of 1907 that Yeats made with Lady Gregory and her son Robert. This opened up new vistas of beauty to him, gave reality to his earlier interest in Italian art, sculpture and literature: Lady Gregory became his Duchess of Urbino, as Maud was his Helen; so Coole became his Urbino.

The third woman is Maud Gonne, her 'eagle look' symbolising nobility and objectivity; he wondered at that constant refusal of hers to waste time discussing herself. 'You know', she told him, 'I hate talking of myself; I am not going to let you make me.'

p. 52, *Fallen Majesty*   This is a poem written in 1912 about Maud Gonne, whose beauty had drawn crowds and, as Yeats recorded in *Autobiographies*, swayed them: when they 'did her bidding they did it not only because she was beautiful but because that beauty suggested joy and freedom'. The 'old men' in the poem suggest the old people in Troy who admired Helen's beauty (Yeats's poem 'When Helen Lived' developed this idea) but the 'even' suggests that some of the older Irish nationalists, such as John O'Leary, who disapproved of Maud's encouragement of violence in the 1890s, found her a charismatic figure. The poem contrasts Maud's withdrawal from politics, at the time Yeats wrote it, with the past, probably those heady days of excitement in 1897 when he travelled with her to various meetings which she addressed with devastating effect.

In addition to the implicit link between Maud and Helen (praised by the blind poet, Homer; see notes on 'The Sorrow of Love', p. 106) created by the mention of the old men (praising beauty, whatever their views about the moral behaviour of its possessor), there is also a suggestion of a link between Maud and the country beauty Mary Hynes (celebrated by the blind Irish poet Raftery). Yeats had spoken to old men and women who remembered her, 'though all are dead now', and they spoke of her as the old men upon the wall of Troy spoke of Helen, 'nor did man or woman differ in their praise'. Helen had her Homer, Mary Hynes her Raftery, and Maud Gonne her Yeats. Crowds may forget, but poetry records beauty and allows it to live on.

p. 52, *A Memory of Youth*   A poem written, probably in August 1912, to Maud Gonne and first entitled 'Love and the Bird'. Yeats later used the image of the stone in 'Easter 1916' to indicate the effect of politics upon Maud: the 'stone of the heart' there indicates what happens to those who give themselves to a cause without thought of their own life or love.

p. 53, *The Two Kings*   A narrative poem of 1912, 'The Two Kings' is probably founded upon *The Yellow Book of Lecan*, *The Book of the Dun Cow* and *The Voyage of Bran*. King Eochaid was High King of Ireland; Tara, County Meath, was the seat of the High Kings. His queen was Edain (see notes on 'The Harp of Aengus', p. 116), who, in the original tales in which she was reborn, married Eochaid who lost a board game to Midhir, King of the Sidhe, who thus won the right to kiss her. Then Midhir and Edain flew out of the smoke-hole of Eochaid's house and returned to the fairy mounds, which Eochaid dug up to get Edain back; she stayed with Midhir, however, Eochaid being tricked into accepting her daughter as his wife. The 'African Mountains of the Moon' are the Ruwenzori in Ruanda. For Ogham, see notes on 'Baile and Aillinn' (p. 117). The Loughlan Waters were Norse waters. Loyal to her human husband, Edain rejects Midhir's advances; in the original tale she returned to the Land of the Gods with him.

p. 59, *A Thought from Propertius*   A poem praising Maud Gonne, which Yeats founded upon the second poem in the second book of Sextus Propertius, the Roman love poet. The descriptions of Maud as 'fit spoil for a centaur' echoes the Latin poem's 'the Centaurs' welcome spoil in the revels'. The link with the Greek goddess Pallas Athene goes back to Yeats's description of Maud Gonne as a goddess in *Autobiographies* and anticipates a late poem, 'Beautiful Lofty Things'.

p. 59, *Her Praise*   A poem written in praise of Maud Gonne in January 1915. Already the war which had been expected to end quickly seems long. Yeats enjoyed using the Irish phrase 'turning the talk', just as he enjoyed directing the conversation and praise upon Maud Gonne.

p. 60, *His Phoenix*   A poem written about Maud Gonne in 1915, comparing her to other women. In the first stanza Yeats uses a word he found in Blake and enjoyed using, 'lineaments', which he applies to a queen who is so unblemished, so white and unstained she could be Leda, loved by Zeus in the form of a swan (see 'Leda and the Swan', p. 77). The reference to the duchesses may be ironic. Yeats had been moving in aristocratic circles in England for some years.

The second stanza lists four women well known on the stage – Gaby Deslys, a French actress and dancer; Ruth St Denis, an American dancer; Anna Matreyevna Pavlova, the Russian ballerina; and Julia Marlowe, an American Shakespearian actress – they too can have their day because he has known Maud in his youth.

The third stanza lists various girlfriends of Ezra Pound, who married Olivia Shakespear's daughter Dorothy in 1914. The fourth stanza concentrates upon Maud's nature. She has been contrasted with a queen, a figure of Greek mythology who mated with a god, with the popular stage figures of the day, and with younger women: she may be equalled by them, but his heart strongly denies it.

p. 61, *A Deep-sworn Vow*   This poem, written in 1915, was prompted by Yeats's thinking that, though Maud had not kept her vow not to marry, and though he had sought consolation elsewhere, he is still obsessed by her.

p. 61, *Broken Dreams*   Another poem written to Maud Gonne which was completed in October 1915 when Yeats was fifty. It shifts from her present appearance to his memories of her as a young woman. The listing of her body's flaw – her small hands were not beautiful – is part of her attractiveness. The unusual in a beloved adds to her uniqueness, a point Yeats made in an essay 'The Tragic Theatre' written five years before this poem.

Complex Harmonies

p. 64, *Owen Aherne and his Dancers*   Yeats married Georgie
Bertha Hyde Lees on 20 October 1917. The first section of this poem
was written on 24 October and the second on 27 October. When first
published in the *Dial* in June 1924, the first section was headed 'The
Lover Speaks', the second 'The Heart Replies'. Owen Aherne, in the
present title, is the name of an invented character (who appears in *The
Tables of the Law* and 'The Phases of the Moon'; here, however, he
seems to be used as a disguise for Yeats himself). The poem records
Yeats's unhappiness; he had first proposed to Maud Gonne's daughter
Iseult in France in 1916 (the year of his last proposal to Maud) and
renewed his efforts to persuade her to marry him in 1917; she finally
refused him when the family came to London – he gave her a week's
ultimatum and he then proposed to Georgie Hyde Lees.

The 'Norman upland' refers to Maud Gonne's household being
situated in Normandy (see notes on 'Peace', p. 122). In the second
section the young child is Iseult (she was born in 1894). Warwick Gould
has suggested that there is an echo here of lines from 'Johnny I hardly
knew you', an old ballad: 'When my poor heart you first beguiled/Why
did you run from me and the child?' The image of the caged bird may
have been suggested by a sardonic remark in a letter from Yeats's
father, the artist John Butler Yeats: 'It is easy to cage the poet bird.
Tennyson was caught and as for Browning he was born in a cage.'

The woman at the poet's side is Mrs Yeats, whose automatic writing
released Yeats's tension and misery. He had begun to think just before
his marriage that he had not acted – as he had believed – for Iseult's sake
rather than his own but because his mind had become unhinged
through strain. Indeed, he considered he had betrayed three people.
George (Mrs Yeats) told him, he wrote on 29 October to Lady Gregory,
that she felt something was to be written through her:

> She got a piece of paper, and talking to me all the while so that her
> thoughts would not affect what she wrote, wrote these words (which she
> did not understand), 'with the bird' (Iseult) 'all is well at heart. Your
> action was right for both but in London you mistook its meaning.'

Within half an hour of the messages being written his fatigue, neuralgia and rheumatic pain were gone; he was extremely happy. He should have said, he added in the letter, that when George had written the sentence he had asked mentally, 'When shall I have peace of mind?' Her hand wrote, 'You will neither regret nor repine,' and he thought he never would again.

p. 65, *Solomon to Sheba*   This is a poem about the poet and his wife written in March 1918. She was then deeply involved in the automatic writing about which Yeats was very excited: it seemed profound, a system of symbolism strange to his wife and to himself, 'a mystical philosophy'; this 'awaited expression', which it got in his *A Vision* (1925; 1937). In the poem Solomon, King of the Hebrews, a figure of wisdom, is used as a symbol for Yeats. Sheba, a ruler in Arabia, in the Yemen, who visited Solomon (see I Kings 10:1-13; the visit is also described, more graphically, in the *Kebra Negast*), suited Mrs Yeats as a symbol - Yeats described his wife as 'strikingly beautiful in a barbaric way'. Yeats considered that the love of Solomon and Sheba must have lasted, despite the silence of the scriptures. True love seemed to him a discipline, for which Solomon and Sheba had the necessary wisdom: 'each derives the secret self of the other, and refusing to believe in the mere daily self, creates a mirror where the lover or the beloved sees an image to copy in daily life; for love also created the mask'.

p. 65, *Solomon and the Witch*   This poem, like 'Solomon to Sheba' about Yeats and his wife (see notes on 'Solomon and Sheba', above), deals with the possibility that the trammels of time may be annihilated, the world having come to a stop, by a perfect union of lovers. The cockerel may be the Hermetic cock, the harbinger of the cycles, in the Tree of Life. It thinks that the end of the dispensation brought in by Eve's eating the 'brigand apple', and thus causing the subsequent Fall of Man, is over, because chance and choice are one.

p. 67, *An Image from a Past Life*   This poem, written in 1919, deals with reincarnation or the presence of past lovers from some past life. The 'hovering thing' of the last line is an Over Shadower or Ideal Form, a form that the lover sees in sleep, a form he or she has loved in some past earthly life. Souls, Yeats wrote in a note in *Michael Robartes and the Dancer*, that are once linked by emotion 'never cease till the last drop of that emotion is exhausted – call it desire, hate, or what you will – to affect one another, remaining always as it were in context'. He added that

> No mind's contents are necessarily shut off from another, and in moments of excitement images pass from one mind to another with extraordinary ease, perhaps most easily from that portion of the mind which for the time being is outside consciousness. I use the word 'pass' because it is familiar, not because I believe any movement in space to be necessary. The second mind sees what the first has already seen, that is all.

He and *She* represent Yeats and his wife, but here they are generalised as lovers or as husband and wife. The scream from beast or bird is associated with moments of revelation. In 'Her Triumph' (p. 80) it comes from a 'miraculous strange bird', and in 'Meditations in Time of Civil War III' Juno's peacock is screaming. The second stanza's lesson is that happiness is not unalloyed, not complete. The fourth stanza, describing the earlier sweetheart from another life, employs language (except for 'arrogant') reminiscent of Yeats's early love poetry to Maud Gonne.

p. 68, *A Prayer for my Daughter*   Yeats's daughter, Anne Butler Yeats, was born in Dublin on 26 February 1919; he began this poem shortly afterwards and it was finished at Thoor Ballylee, Yeats's tower in County Galway, in the following June. 'Gregory's wood' refers to Coole Park, Lady Gregory's estate, near which the tower was situated.

The poet thinks that Helen, associated in his mind with Maud Gonne, found married life with Menelaus in Sparta dull, and so had much trouble from running away with Paris (see notes on 'The Sorrow of Love', p. 106). Aphrodite (fatherless, because she was born of the sea), though a beautiful goddess, married the lame smith Hephaestus; she, like Helen, was forced into adultery, in her case with Ares, the god of war. Both women spoiled their lives, which were plenteously endowed; the 'Horn of Plenty' is the cornucopia, one of the goat Amalthea's horns: she suckled Zeus, father of the Greek gods, and when the horn broke off she gave it to him; it flowed with nectar and ambrosia. Next Yeats, the 'poor man that has roved,/Loved and thought himself beloved', praises courtesy and charm; he cannot take his eyes from his wife's glad kindness. There is probably a natural shift from his own restless moving about to a wish that his daughter may live, like a laurel tree, 'Rooted in one dear perpetual place', the image of the linnet reminding us of the linnet's wings in 'The Lake Isle of Innisfree', which in his youth in London seemed an idyllic place. He thinks of how the minds and beauty he has loved are faring badly – Maud Gonne had been in Holloway gaol – and sees the dangers of hate, returning to the image of the linnet, considering that it will be unharmed while a mind has no hatred. This meditation upon hatred turns to a savage condemnation of Maud Gonne – born, like Helen and Aphrodite, out of plenty's horn – who has, because of her opinionated hatreds, bartered that horn 'For an old bellows full of angry wind'. The poem ends on a happier note, praising innocence, custom and ceremony, returning to the images of the horn of plenty and the laurel tree.

p. 71, *The Gift of Harun Al-Rashid*   This poem pays tribute to the poet's wife, to her beauty, learning and psychic gifts. The poem is based upon Yeats's reading the *Arabian Nights*. Harun Al-Rashid was Caliph from 786 to 809. Kusta ben Luka, a doctor and translator, lived from 820 to (?)892. A note in *The Cat and the Moon and Certain Poems* (1924) gives a humorous, indirect account of how Mrs Yeats's automatic writing had given her husband the material for *A Vision*. In this, Harun Al-Rashid presents Kusta (who symbolises Yeats) with a new bride. According to one tradition of the desert, she had, to the surprise of her friends, fallen in love with the elderly philosopher (Yeats, born on 20 June 1865, was fifty-two when he married Georgie Hyde Lees, born on 17 October 1892, who was twenty-six), but, according to another tradition, Harun bought her from a passing merchant. One version of the story said that Kusta, who was, like the physician of the Caliph, a Christian, planned to end his days in a monastery; another, however, had it that he was deeply involved 'in a violent love affair that he had arranged for himself'. He had, it was generally agreed, been warned in a dream to accept the Caliph's gift, and a few days after their marriage his wife began to talk in her sleep.

She told him 'all those things which he had searched for vainly all his life in the great library of the Caliph and in the conversation of wise men'.

Parmenides, the founder of the Eleatic school of philosophy, regarded the universe as unchanging. Jaffer was Vizier from 780 to 803, when the Caliph ordered his imprisonment. The remark 'If but the shirt upon my body knew it/I'd tear it off and throw it in the fire' comes, Warwick Gould suggests, from Powys Mathers's translation of the *Arabian Nights*, published in 1923: 'If I thought my shirt knew I would tear my shirt in pieces'.

The bride is praised because she shared Kusta ben Luka's thirst for those 'old crabbed mysteries' (Georgie Hyde Lees had joined the Order of the Golden Dawn before their marriage; she was well read in the occult tradition). A Djinn is a supernatural being; the Yeatses spoke of the mystical beings who transmitted their messages through Mrs Yeats's writing as 'communicators'. The account of Kusta's bride marking emblems in the desert sand derives from 'King Wird Khan, his Women and his Wazirs', in Burton's translation of the *Arabian Nights*; in this, Wird Khan, in disguise, asks a boy how he knows State secrets. He replies that he knows from the sand 'wherewith I take comfort of night and day and from the sayings of the ancients'. His father had taught him geomancy. The boy shows that he is sagacious and is rewarded with the wazirship.

p. 77, *Leda and the Swan*   In Greek myth, Leda, the wife of Tyndareus, King of Sparta, was bathing in the river Eurotas when Zeus saw her. He took the shape of a swan and coupled with her. From this union of god and mortal woman were born Castor and Pollux and Helen, through whom the Trojan War came about (see notes on 'The Sorrow of Love', p. 106). That war is evoked economically, with the wall broken to admit the wooden horse, the sack of the city, the tower (perhaps that from which Astyanax, the infant son of Hector snatched from his mother Andromache, was thrown to his death by the Greeks) and Agamemnon, murdered on his return to Argos by Clytaemnestra (a daughter of Leda by her husband Tyndareus) and her lover Aegisthus.

The poem ponders whether Leda assumed any of Zeus's knowledge;

in their union Yeats saw the annunciation of Greek civilisation. When asked for a poem for the *Irish Statesman* by the editor, his friend George Russell, he had begun to think about the movement of European political thought. After the writings of Hobbes, the Encyclopaedists and the ensuing French Revolution, he considered the soil exhausted, nothing possible but some movement, or birth from above, preceded by a violent annunciation (the theme of his famous poem of this period, 'The Second Coming'). He began to play with the metaphor of Leda and the Swan, but, as he wrote, 'bird and lady took such possession of the scene that all politics went out of it, and my friend tells me that his conservative readers would misunderstand the poem'.

From 'A Woman Young and Old'

With one exception, not included in this section, the poems grouped under this title by Yeats were written in 1926 and 1927. They are arranged here in Yeats's sequence. He wrote them in the following order: 'Chosen', 'A Last Confession', 'Parting', 'Her Vision in the Wood', 'Her Triumph' and 'Consolation'.

p. 80, *Her Triumph*   This is a poem written in 1926. In 'Michael Robartes and the Dancer', written in 1918, Yeats had been influenced by a picture ascribed to Bordone in the National Gallery of Ireland, *Saint George and the Dragon*. He had also seen Cosimo Tura's *St. George and the Dragon* in Ferrara Cathedral in 1907. 'A pagan Perseus' may have been suggested by Perino del Vaga's *Andromeda and Perseus*, of which Yeats had a reproduction. Perseus was the son of Zeus and Danaë (whom Zeus had visited in a shower of gold), the daughter of Acrisius, King of Argos, whom Perseus later killed by mistake. Andromeda, daughter of Cepheus, King of Ethiopia, and Cassiopeia, was rescued from a dragon by Perseus, who also killed Medusa the Gorgon. The image of the 'miraculous strange bird' may derive from William Morris, 'The Doom of King Acrisius', in *The Earthly Paradise*.

p. 80, *Consolation*   This is a poem of June 1927. The phrase 'the crime of being born' is echoed in 'the crime of death and birth' in 'A Dialogue of Self and Soul', a poem largely written between July and December 1927, and completed in spring 1928.

p. 81, *Chosen*   This poem, probably written early in 1926, uses the arrangement of rhymes Yeats found in John Donne's 'A Nocturnal upon St. Lucies Day'. The idea of love being chosen may come from Plato's myth of Er, in which men and women in heaven choose the lots of their future destinies. The sun progresses through the whirling Zodiac and Yeats symbolised a woman's love as 'the struggle of the darkness to keep the sun from rising from its earthly bed'. In this poem's second stanza he changed the symbol, he commented in his first note to the poem, to that of 'the souls of man and woman ascending through the Zodiac'. This note was expanded: the learned astrologer was Ambrosius Theodosius Macrobius, and the reference is to his comment on Scipio's Dream, that 'when the sun is in Aquarius . . . it is in the sign inimical to human life; and from thence, the meeting place of the Zodiac and Milky Way, the descending soul by its defluction is drawn out of the spherical, the sole divine form, into the cone'. The miraculous stream of the poem is the Milky Way. The sphere relates to the Thirteenth Sphere, or Cone, in *A Vision*.

p. 81, *Parting*   This poem, written in August 1928, echoes, according to Joseph Hone, the fifth scene of the third act of *Romeo and Juliet* where the lovers argue over whether it is daylight, whether they have heard the nightingale or the lark. Romeo thinks it was the lark and he must 'be gone and live, or stay and die'.

p. 82, *Her Vision in the Wood*   Written in 1928, this poem probably portrays, through the wounded man and the beast, the Greek legend of Adonis, a beautiful young man whom Aphrodite loved; he was killed by a wild boar and the anemone was said to have sprung from his blood. Persephone restored him to life on condition that he spent six months of the year with her and six with Aphrodite. His death and revival were celebrated in various festivals and he seems to have been a winter–summer symbol. Yeats may, however, have had in mind, according to T. R. Henn, Diarmuid, the Irish hero who was killed by a boar on Ben Bulben, a Sligo mountain (see notes on 'He mourns for the Change that has come upon him and his Beloved, and longs for the End of the World', p. 113). The comparison of the women to 'a Quattrocento painter's throng' is apposite. Andrea Mantegna was an Italian painter born near Vicenza in 1431.

p. 83, *A Last Confession*   This poem was written between June and August 1926. The bird image appears in 'A Memory of Youth' (p. 52) and 'Her Triumph' (p. 80; see note, p. 133).

From 'A Man Young and Old'

These poems were written between 1926 and 1927, a companion series to *A Woman Young and Old*. It is not possible to date their composition precisely; they are arranged in the order in which Yeats placed them.

p. 86, *First Love*   This poem is about the effect of Maud Gonne on the poet. The 'heart of stone' in the second stanza echoes 'a stone of the heart' in 'Easter 1916'; it is an image for those who devote all their being to a cause.

p. 86, *Human Dignity*   This poem deals with Yeats's frustrated love for Maud Gonne. In his diary for 22 January 1909 he wrote that she never understood his plans or ideas, but consoled himself with the query of how much of the best he had done and still did was 'but the attempt to explain myself to her'. If she understood he would have no reason for writing and 'one can never have too many reasons for doing what is laborious'.

p. 87, *The Mermaid*   This poem is a vignette of Yeats's affair with Olivia Shakespear in 1896. Warwick Gould suggests that the image comes from George Moore's novel *Evelyn Innes* (1896), in which the main character, Ulick Dean, modelled on Yeats, kissed Evelyn Innes, who threw her arms about his neck 'and drew him down as a mermaid draws her mortal lover into the depths'.

p. 87, *The Empty Cup*   This poem, too, refers to Yeats's affair with Olivia Shakespear. 'One looks back to one's youth', he wrote to her on 6 December 1926, 'as to [a] cup that a madman dying of thirst left half tasted. I wonder if you feel like that?' The story of how Olivia realised (in 1897) that Maud was still deep in Yeats's heart is told in the poem 'The Lover mourns for the Loss of Love':

> *Pale hands, still hands and dim hair,*
> *I had a beautiful friend*
> *And dreamed that the old despair*
> *Would end in love in the end:*
> *She looked in my heart one day*
> *And saw your image was there;*
> *She has gone weeping away.*

p. 88, *His Memories*   A poem reverting to Homeric personae. Hector, the brave son of Priam, King of Troy, was happily married to Andromache; the description of his farewell to her and their son Astyanax is one of the most haunting passages in Homer's *Iliad*. 'The first of all the tribe' is Helen, who caused the fall of Troy: she is usually used as a symbol for Maud Gonne (see notes on 'The Sorrow of Love', p. 106). The poem may indicate that Yeats did (possibly in 1908 or 1910) sleep with Maud.

From 'Words for Music Perhaps'

Yeats wrote many of the poems of *Words for Music Perhaps* between 1929 and 1931. He had been seriously ill, and wrote in his introduction to *The Winding Stair* (1929) that life had returned to him 'as an impression of the uncontrollable energy and daring of the great creators'. He called the group of poems *Words for Music Perhaps* in memory of those 'exultant weeks' when he wrote most of the poems. They are arranged here in the order of their composition.

p. 90, *Lullaby*   In this poem, written in March 1929 and described to Olivia Shakespear as a mother singing to her child, Yeats depicts three sets of lovers: Paris and Helen, Tristram and Iseult, and Zeus and Leda. For Paris and Helen see notes on 'The Sorrow of Love' (p. 106), and 'Peace' (p. 122). Tristram, 'the son of the King of Lyonesse' in Malory's *Le Morte d'Arthur*, was sent to Ireland to be cured of a wound. There he fell in love with La Beale Isoud, the King's daughter. On his return to Cornwall he was told by King Mark to go back to Ireland to ask La Beale Isoud to marry King Mark. She agreed, but remained in love with Tristram; they had unwittingly drunk a love potion. Subsequently they were betrayed to Mark and Tristram left Mark's court. There are two versions of his death. The 'holy bird', in the third stanza, is the form taken by Zeus in his affair with Leda (see notes on 'Leda and the Swan', p. 132).

p. 90, *Young Man's Song*   This is a poem written after March 1929, which resembles 'Before the World was made', a poem written a little over a year earlier, in which a girl looks for the face she had, an archetypal one. The idea may be derived from Plato's myth of Er (see notes on 'Chosen', p. 134). The phrase 'bend the knee' was common in nineteenth-century Irish political oratory.

p. 91, *After Long Silence*   This poem, written in November 1929, is about Yeats's youthful relationship with Olivia Shakespear.

p. 91, *Crazy Jane on God*   The earthy character Crazy Jane was founded upon 'Cracked Mary', who lived in a cottage near Gort, County Galway. Yeats described her as the local satirist, 'audacious in her outspoken speech'. In this poem, written on 18 July 1931, Crazy Jane puts the view that sexual love is a passing thing. She also shows herself aware that some things survive. Battles can be relived, or passionate moments. The imagery of the men-at-arms may have been suggested by Cracked Mary, who saw 'unearthly' riders on white horses. (Mary Battle, a servant of Yeats's uncle George Pollexfen, who lived in Sligo, also saw superhuman figures on horseback on the mountainside. There are several places in Ireland where the sounds of battles being fought – usually on their anniversaries – are reported to have been heard.) The image of the empty, ruined house being suddenly lit up was used by Yeats in other places: in 'The Curse of Cromwell' and in the plays *The King of the Great Clock Tower* and *Purgatory*. It may have been a memory of an Irish countrywoman saying she had seen the ruined Castle Dargan (in County Sligo) 'lit up'.

p. 92, *Crazy Jane and Jack the Journeyman*   This poem was written in November 1931. The two invented characters appeared in the first Crazy Jane poem, 'Crazy Jane and the Bishop', written in March 1929, Jack the Journeyman being a contrasting character to the Bishop who had, when younger, denounced Jane and Jack as living together 'like beast and beast'.

p. 93, *Crazy Jane talks with the Bishop*   The poem, written in November 1931, may owe something to Villon's 'An Old Woman's Lamentation', which John Millington Synge translated. A line in Blake's *Jerusalem*, 'For I will make their place of love and joy excrementitious', probably prompted the assertion that 'Love has pitched his mansion in/The place of excrement'.

Testimonies of Later Years

p. 96, *Coole and Ballylee, 1931*   Yeats wrote two fine poems about his dear friend Lady Gregory and her house: the first was 'Coole Park, 1929' which praised 'a woman's powerful character'. This second poem was written in February 1931 when Lady Gregory was old and ill. It moves from Yeats's nearby tower at Ballylee, from the river with its associations with the blind Irish poet Raftery to the flooded lake at Coole, touching upon water, seen as a symbol of generation by the Neoplatonists, and particularly Porphyry. The swan which rises from the lake is an image of inspiration – the idea of its being murdered by a spot of ink comes from *Le Docteur Tribulat Bonhomet* (1887), a novel by the French symbolist Count Villiers de l'Isle-Adam, in which Dr Bonhomet is a hunter of swans. Then the poet turns to Lady Gregory, 'a last inheritor' (for her son Robert was killed in the First

World War; Yeats wrote several poems about him, notably 'In Memory of Major Robert Gregory' and 'An Irish Airman Foresees his Death'), describing her in the great house so full of the past, rich because of its stability. 'We were the last romantics', he declares with bravura, but he measures the decline. The poet's steed Pegasus is riderless now, and the flood is darkening.

p. 97, *Quarrel in Old Age*   This poem, written in November 1931, records a quarrel with Maud Gonne, probably over the treatment of women prisoners on hunger strike. The 'blind bitter town' is Dublin, so characterised in the earlier poems of *Responsibilities* and in the later poem 'Words'. In the last line Yeats returns to an earlier idea, put in *Autobiographies* in his account of their first meeting, that Maud Gonne, targeted (protected by a round shield or targe), seemed 'like a classical impersonation of the spring'.

p. 98, *Ribh at the Tomb of Baile and Aillinn*   In this poem, completed by 24 July 1934, Ribh is an invented character, an old hermit; his thought echoes pre-Christian ideas, Yeats commented; his Christianity came perhaps from Egypt. Baile and Aillinn were the lovers whose story is told in 'The Withering of the Boughs' and in 'Baile and Aillinn' (p. 37). A yew tree grew where Baile was buried, an apple over Aillinn: their love stories were written in boards made of yew and apple. The 'intercourse of angels' came from Swedenborg's remark that 'the sexual intercourse of angels is a conflagration of the whole being'. The circular light of the conflagration in the poem may indicate the perfect harmony of the lovers.

p. 99, *Margot*   This poem, unpublished in Yeats's lifetime, was written to Margot Ruddock, whom he met in 1934 when she was twenty-seven; she asked him to help her in creating a poet's theatre. Ruddock was her maiden name; she was divorced from Jack Collis and married Raymond Lovell in 1932. Yeats wrote a foreword for her poems in *The Lemon Tree* (1937), and *Ah, Sweet Dancer, W. B. Yeats, Margot Ruddock. A Correspondence* (1970), edited by Roger McHugh, shows the course of their relationship. Yeats wrote her several poems, among them those published in *New Poems* (1938), 'Sweet Dancer' and 'A Crazed Girl'.

p. 99, *The Spur*   This poem, written in December 1936, Yeats called his 'final apology' in a letter to Dorothy Wellesley.

p. 100, *The Three Bushes*   This poem was written in July 1935. Its source, supposedly an incident in the Abbé Michel de Bourdeille's *Historia mei Temporis*, was a piece of invention. (There was a Pierre de Bourdeilles, abbot and Lord of Brantôme, who lived from 1527–1614.) Yeats, however, derived the poem from a ballad by Dorothy Wellesley. The poem's history, as well as that of their friendship, can be read in *Letters on Poetry from W. B. Yeats to Dorothy Wellesley* (1940).

p. 102, *The Lady's First Song*   This poem, written in November 1936, is part of the sequence of poems built around 'The Three Bushes' (p. 100), the drama of which Yeats thought it would heighten. The imagery is reminiscent of 'A Last Confession' (p. 83).

p. 103, *A Bronze Head*   This poem, probably written in 1937 or 1938, was prompted by Laurence Campbell's plaster-cast painted bronze of Maud Gonne MacBride 'at right of the entrance' to the Municipal Gallery of Modern Art in Dublin.

   Yeats's reference to the 'tomb-haunter' probably indicates the habit Maud Gonne had of attending funerals where the person being buried had political significance: in old age she constantly wore long, black, flowing clothes and a veil. '*Hysterica passio*' is hysteria and probably derives from *King Lear*, act 2, scene iv: 'Hysterica passio, down, thou climbing sorrow'. Yeats invokes the Cambridge philosopher J. McT. E. McTaggart, who argues for the compound nature of all substances. The supernatural element in the last stanza may have been suggested by some of McTaggart's views in *Immortality and Pre-existence* (1915).

p. 104, *Politics*   Written in May 1938, this poem was Yeats's response to 'Public Speech and Private Speech in Poetry', an article by Archibald MacLeish in the *Yale Review*, which contained the quotation from Thomas Mann that Yeats used as an epigraph. He liked MacLeish's article, which praised his language as public but argued that Yeats, owing to his age and his relation to Ireland, was unable to use this public language 'on what it considered the right material – politics'.

INDEX TO TITLES

INDEX TO FIRST LINES